LOST IN CANADA

LOST IN CANADA

An Immigrant's Second Thoughts

LYDIA PEROVIĆ

sh.
SUTHERLAND
HOUSE
TORONTO, 2022

Sutherland House
416 Moore Ave., Suite 205
Toronto, ON M4G 1C9

Sutherland House and logo are registered trademarks of The Sutherland House Inc.

First edition, April 2022

If you are interested in inviting one of our authors to a live event or media appearance, please contact sranasinghe@sutherlandhousebooks.com and visit our website at sutherlandhousebooks.com for more information about our authors and their schedules.

Manufactured in the Canada
Cover designed by Lena Yang
Book composed by Karl Hunt

Library and Archives Canada Cataloguing in Publication
Title: Lost in Canada : an immigrant's second thoughts / Lydia Perovic.
Names: Perović, Lydia, 1974- author.
Identifiers: Canadiana 2022016505X |
ISBN 9781989555576 (softcover)
Subjects: LCSH: Perović, Lydia, 1974- |
LCSH: Immigrants—Canada—Biography. | LCSH: Authors,
Canadian—21st century—Biography. | CSH: Authors,
Canadian (English)—21st century—Biography |
LCGFT: Autobiographies.
Classification: LCC PS8631.E7345 Z46 2022 |
DDC C813/.6—dc23

ISBN 978-1989555576

Wouldn't we rather have a destiny to submit to, then, something that claims us, anything, instead of such flimsy choices, arbitrary days?

Alice Munro, 'Albanian Virgin'

Chapter 1

At the midpoint on the journey of life, I found myself in a dark forest, for the clear path was lost.

O R TO GIVE my own riff on Dante, after twenty uncomplicated years of living as an adopted Canadian, I find myself in a dark forest, for the belonging is lost.

I used to have it: I have been saying *we* easily for almost two decades. I moved here from the 1990s wars in the Western Balkans as a graduate student to escape the relentless history of home, and in search of a functioning draft of a liberal democracy. Here, to the country that doesn't quite gel, is decentralized into smithereens and interrupted with enormous empty spaces, none of which particularly disturbs it. Where mutual differences are vast and we'd rather not overanalyze what they mean, just live pretending that they don't exist. Blandness: behind it is an uneventful competence in governance, fundamentally Red Tory political instincts (meaning, easy-does-it, conformist, communitarian—at least until the neoliberal era, and figures like Mike Harris and Paul Martin).[1] Fair play as an agreed-upon ideal. And very little history.

After the Balkans, it's what I wanted. Explaining where I'm from is nearly impossible. Today it's called Montenegro. Before that it was SFR Yugoslavia, the Kingdom of Serbs, Croats and Slovenes, the Kingdom and Principality of Montenegro, the Austro-Hungarian Empire, Napoleonic France, Venice, the Principality of Zeta, the Ottoman Empire, the Byzantine Empire, further back the Roman Empire, and further back still the Illyrians . . . But this exercise in phantom roots is tiresome. A nation is not blood and soil; it is a moral conscience, "having made great things together and wishing to make them again," wrote the French historian Ernest Renan. A "great solidarity" with the past and the future; a daily plebiscite.

Canada, with its declared agnosticism about blood and belonging— agnosticism that came through the front door officially with Pierre Elliott Trudeau but had many earlier traces—is of the Enlightenment, although by birthday of its confederation she is rather Victorian. The person writing these lines also understood herself to be a child of the Enlightenment, intent on proving with her own life that we can abandon blind obedience to traditions and re-examine our life and everything we've known, and become part of a new society—community even—based on shared ideals and the conscious choice to belong. Now she is not sure anymore that that's how things work.

Something's been happening with the *we*. I am beginning to suspect that there are fewer and fewer of us believing in the "great solidarity" across ethnicity, class, and time.

---

1   All the notes and references are at the end of book.

My adoptive country and my city are becoming unrecognizable. Conversations in the public sphere are changing, as are those in the media and the culture. Public speech increasingly must be premised with a recitation of pronouns—this is now even required of lawyers before B.C.courts and their clients—and land acknowledgements. What should those who do not share those religious and ideological beliefs do? Are we always already letting the side down even before we've said anything? The internet speaks American and so, increasingly, do we, importing wholesale the culture wars as they happen in the US, adopting the diagnoses of American problems as universally relevant. There is this elaborate vocabulary of political contestation all around us, why not use it? the thinking goes. We apply the American framework of irreconcilable 'black' and 'white' difference to Canada and harden the settler and Indigenous split. Where this paradigm is not available, the cleaving is along the lines of 'white' and 'BIPOC,' a strange acronym unifying all Black, Indigenous and people of colour, as if they all have something in common, as if not being 'white' automatically groups them into the same category.

Over the last five years in particular, people running Canadian cultural institutions and media have put all of their chips on irreconcilable differences. There is no Canada for all, no political cause for all, and no arts for all. There is no individual outside ethnic determinism: there are bits and bobs of inter-regional and inter-ethnic resentment. What happens to class analysis under those circumstances? What happens to arts? Art criticism? The possibility of "great solidarity?" Freedom of expression?

Free speech used to be a liberal-left cause when *The Body Politic* magazine existed, Little Sister's bookstore had its literature stopped at the Canada-US border, NDP MP Svend Robinson questioned the need to refer to a God in the Canadian constitution, and further back, when Manitoba's United College fired Prof. Harry Crowe over an expressed political opinion, the NDP opposed the War Measures Act, Doris Anderson edited *Chatelaine*, and further back still, when William Lyon Mackenzie was publishing the *Colonial Advocate*. Freedom of speech is not a top-drawer value for the left and liberal centre in Canada any longer. I'll be looking at the irreconcilable difference, the weariness about freedom of expression, and the inching toward illiberalism in the first chapter.

It's not just that Canada has forgotten it used to think of itself as a liberal democracy. Illiberalism in the chattering classes is one thing. Sometimes liberalism leaves the society open to illiberal developments by its own constitution. It shies away from questions about a good, fulfilled life worth living, and limits itself to offering one type of freedom—freedom from interference—and not giving enough space to positive freedom, the capacity building and real options for its citizens. I live in a city, and a country, where car drivers and house owners decide what living in the city and country is going to be like for everybody. Where only those who are upper-middle class (and up) can give a career in the arts, literature, or journalism a go. Where only citizens with that kind of solvency can count on having consistent access to psychotherapy.

Toronto 2022 is a hybrid of Dubai (endless luxury condominium towers) and Vancouver (extreme housing costs). It's also a place of people who are compelled to work and hustle more than ever, who have stopped reading books, are screen-bound, and increasingly lonely. If a certain liberal and democratic mettle is necessary for liberal democracy to be accomplished and carried over into the future, do we have enough of it? Can that political ideal survive without the kind of citizens who can be relied on to have a degree of independence of spirit, curiosity, capacity for deep concentration, and freedom from fear and penury? In chapters two through seven I tackle these snags. What do we do with the idea of Canadian culture as it recedes on the horizon? If citizens of a nation are not particularly interested in its film and literature, will they be interested in its other features? Electoral politics, foreign affairs, what the PMO is up to, or city council?

Chapter eight tries to confront what is possibly the most uprooting event of anybody's life.

From chapter nine on, my first country, Montenegro, joins the conversation: its narratives, history, the wars of the 1990s, and its unexpected presence in the fiction of one of Canada's most celebrated writers. Discovering the reverse, the presence of Canada in Montenegrin culture, was equally unexpected. I have been trying to re-establish some of my ties to Montenegro and the South Slavic region because I severed them too radically, thinking that was freedom and that it was necessary. But this enterprise proved to be bizarrely hard: after a twenty-year absence, I might as well be a New Caledonian. A lapsed Montenegrin will have as difficult a time growing roots and finding gainful employment in her old country as would a visitor from the southern hemisphere. But fiction and narrative arts are doing their thing, weaving tendrils across the ocean, alleviating my neurosis over being split. *Only connect.* And sometimes, to my astonishment, I succeed.

There's a vintage shop in the east end of Toronto that I used to frequent called Gadabout. It sells everything old, but I went for the drawers upon drawers brimming with postcards and black and white family photos. (Both, I presume, are resupplied whenever an elderly Toronto resident dies and the offspring or some stranger clean the apartment and remove the belongings.) The vintage postcards I brought home and sorted by decade. They might begin with the start of the twentieth century and end with the sixties; the changes in style and topics of depiction from one decade to next easy to spot. I also own a few of somebody's old family photos, and I used to have a private art project where I mixed them with my own family photos from the same era, or put them on the wall as a group. On one wall of my previous apartment in Toronto's Junction neighbourhood, I hung the hand-written land purchasing agreement of 1900 from the city of Ulcinj, principality of Montenegro, next to a photo of an unknown Toronto family of nine arranged on the porch of a brick house, dressed in their Edwardian best. Same time, different geographies.

The project has for some time now moved from card shuffling and wall decoration to real life. The pondering of belonging has moved from the head to the whole body: aging, childlessness, the possibility of a non-biological family and friendship between women, the unused time with parents, which can never be retrieved. What could a nation still mean and is it a kind of solidarity that we should keep alive in our lives? With this book, I adamantly say yes, although my younger self would be surprised by my answer. In the middle of my life, I find myself a stranger to my old country, while my new country of twenty years of uncomplicated belonging suddenly also looks strange and impermeable. When we are nowhere, when we don't know where we are, that's where the thinking begins, that's where writing starts, said psychoanalyst Julia Kristeva (from her stable, accomplished, married, bourgeois life in France). While I used to believe that, I'm not so sure anymore. But let's get into it.

Chapter 2

FAR FROM TORONTO'S DOWNTOWN, in the land of sub-
divisions, six-lane traffic and strip malls around Lawrence
Ave. East and Bellamy Rd., sits one of the oldest cemeteries in
North America. The grass of the modest municipal park named Tabor
Hill covers the ossuary of the Huron-Wendat people dating back to the
pre-contact 1300s. Ossuaries like this one were built during the ten-day
festival of the dead, as described in the 1600s by the French Jesuit settler
to Nouvelle France Jean de Brébeuf and centuries later confirmed by
modern archaeology. When a Huron village depleted its resources, they'd
move to another location, taking their temporarily buried relatives with
them. (It won't be hard to guess which of the two sexes had the duty to
clean the remains and prepare them for the passage.) On some occasions,
several villages would gather to build one common burial ground. As they
did on Tabor Hill.

Far from here, over in New France, the Huron had invited Brébeuf
to join the bones of the deceased French to the buried Huron, a nation-
building act *avant la lettre*, perhaps from an intuition of a multi-confessional

society lying ahead. Being a Catholic, Brébeuf could not imagine that in the course of the Second Coming, the Saviour, coming across one such ossuary, would be even remotely able to handpick the saved from the infidels for the purposes of the resurrection of flesh, and gave it a pass.

The Huron Feast of the Souls petered out as a practice over time, and the Huron confederacy dispersed. The decline was partly due to diseases brought over by Europeans, but the wars with another Indigenous group, the Iroquois/Haudenosaunee, are also to blame. (The Tabor Hill plaque, in one of those ironies that historical mappings are rife with, indicates that the ossuary was Iroquois, but following the discovery by the city archaeologists that it actually belonged to the Huron, the plaque was never updated.) The conflicts and differences among the Indigenous peoples preceded the European arrival, and the rivalries were exacerbated by the fur trade and the general jostling for resources and territories among the colonies. Sides were taken, alliances formed. Indigenous groups fought on different sides in The Seven Years' War between the French and the British, and they fought on the side of British North America in the wars of 1812 against the American republic. Canada's first peoples have been as unified a world-historical subject as the Europeans have been – in other words, not at all.

Therefore, the land acknowledgements recited before practically all cultural and education events in Toronto as of late do not quite tell the whole truth. "We acknowledge that this event takes place on the lands occupied for centuries by the peoples X, Y, and Z and we are grateful to them to be here" obscures the fact that possession of the land was contested among those groups and moreover, the land was not owned in any way that property is owned today or back then. Land acknowledgements are a collective saying of grace, in effect, while they teach no history, and do nothing to improve actual Indigenous lives. Yet they are everywhere. I once attended a Liederabend which began with the young soloist asking the audience to read aloud the land acknowledgment projected for them on the subtitles screen. A theatre season launch opened with a ten-minute smudging ceremony, the context or the purpose of which was never explained. Saying grace before unrelated events – in performance of atonement, validation? – is just one of the aspects of the process called 'Indigenization' ('reconciliation', itself vague and pious, is no longer enough) in the public sphere that old-stock Anglophone Canadians have embraced with unusual ardour.

Granted, as a person from the western Balkans I could be unusually uncomfortable with talk of one's ethnicity having a special relationship to a land, because the pursuit of that political idea has been ravaging my continent of origin for millennia. When I complained on Twitter about having to observe mandatory smudging ceremonies at opera season launches, a Twitter activist asked me why I don't go back to where the rituals that I find meaningful connect me to the land where I am from. It's becoming increasingly difficult to talk to Canadian progressives if talk of blood and belonging, and rituals specific to a stretch of land, is not your thing.

The Twitter activist in question, by the way, was not from around here either: she grew up on the west coast of Canada, among very different Indigenous groups than the ones that live in the old Canada of Ontario and Quebec. What do all the first peoples have in common, exactly? Languages are different, weather and geography are different, and the degree of interest in being integrated into liberal democratic procedures and capitalist production varies among groups. And these differences, as the Wet'suwet'en case recently showed, sometimes exist between the elected and hereditary representatives within the same nation.

A further thing is obscured by land acknowledgement: many, probably all, Indigenous rights advocates and 'representatives' of indigeneity in culture, including the most vocal ones, are a mix of western European and Indigenous parentage, making them more Western European and WASP or Celtic than the Slav writing these lines. But the 'Indigeneity' takes primacy in personal history, to align with the person's politics, to fit in the dominant mode of political contestation of the era.

The current generation of Indigenous rights activists would find my argument hard to compute. The division of Settler vs. Indigenous has sharpened, conceptually and politically, in recent years as much as the division of black vs. white in the US. Effectively, peoples who have little in common are imagined as one ethnicity (the non-Settler) inhabiting one economic position (reduced to poverty by past and ongoing colonization), and possessed of one possible psyche (traumatized by past and ongoing colonization, permanently devoid of agency over its life story, resulting in higher addiction and mental health issues). While conversations to the south have many notable dissidents from the "all-American skin game" and "racecraft" (including Thomas Chatterton Williams, Kmele Foster, John McWhorter, Chloé Valdary, Glenn Loury, Coleman Hughes and many more), there are virtually no progressives north of the border who attempt to argue that the impoverished Indigenous and the immigrant precariat have more in common with each other than either of us have with the well-offs of our own ethnic cohort. Or, to put it more broadly, that Canada is one country, to which people from around the world emigrate to escape ethnic and religious over-determination—a project very much worth keeping alive.

'Indigenization' is a value adopted by a growing number of institutions. What does that look like, apart from land acknowledgements? A few examples. Mandatory Indigenous-themed content in education, and if this happens to clash with academic freedoms, too bad for academic freedoms. It's quite legal to restrict academic job openings in Canada to certain ethnic groups or under-represented demographics. A project to 'decolonize physics' got a lot of government funding recently. A part-Indigenous, part-South Asian playwright asked the Toronto media not to send a "white" critic to review her play; many in the theatre world applauded, and a national newspaper sort of complied (they sent an additional, ethnically-correct critic alongside their usual one). The Canada Council for the Arts recently hired an Indigenous activist-journalist as its chair. His goal? To reduce "the harm" inflicted by pesky colonizing arts grants.

Meanwhile, in literature, writers are terrified of accusations of cultural appropriation, of getting into the same pickle as Angie Abdou, a writer who followed the prescribed procedures for writing about an Indigenous group in fiction, and was still found wanting, criticized by her WASP peers and Indigenous groups alike. The long-term effect of this tension will shape up as two separate literatures, one legitimately Indigenous, and one for the rest of Canada, devoid of Indigenous characters. Some competitions for writers-in-residence already advertise that they are open to "Canadian and Indigenous writers." Works like *Louis Riel*, Harry Somers' and Mavor Moore's modernist masterwork opera, would not be funded or made today, nor would Margaret Atwood be able to write the libretto for *Pauline,* a chamber opera about the Indigenous writer Pauline Johnson.

This paradigm also feeds a booming educational-legal-media industry which profits off the othering of Indigenous peoples: interpreting what they are, what they want, what they are entitled to, and how they are fundamentally different from everybody else in Canada.

The Supreme Court ruled in the mid-1970s that the country will entertain new land claims, and the ensuing activism led to a state of affairs where the majority of the culturati and progressive media understands the country as existing on a bunch of unceded territories, akin to a random drawing on a napkin. The nation-to-nation rhetoric is gaining in strength, bolstered by Prime Minister Justin Trudeau's government.

Has the increasing separateness of Indigenous peoples in the Canadian project made their lives better? They are still overrepresented in femicide stats, suicide stats, and incarceration, and disproportionately affected by the lack of basic infrastructure on self-governing reserves. Now that separateness has been tried, would somebody please advocate for more closeness and more belonging, so that these societal problems are understood for what they are: problems that *we* as a country and *our* children (not *they* and *their* children) are facing?

Because we do share a lot of problems. The writer Sherman Alexie once said that immigrants and the Indigenous share much in common. Structurally, we're outside the dominant culture, with similar problems of belonging. But when I say we share a lot of problems, I mean all of us, the Canadian-born as well. Our national economy relies too much on resource extraction and US exports. We work too much for what we earn—we work too much period—at jobs that don't fulfill most of us. The value of the arts in our lives is diminishing. We read fewer books, and make fewer friends. We often cocoon in our own ethnic groups. We can't really navigate our cities without an automobile. We are dependent on American screens. We know more about American politics and culture than our own. Especially in urban centres, we find it harder and harder to pay our rents and mortgages.

In Toronto, in particular, I would argue that the greatest divide is not between the sexes or the races, but between the owners and the renters. It *is* all about the land in one of the most expensive cities in North America, but not in the way we believe. Most of Toronto is taken up by what city planners call the yellow belt, single-family houses with back and front yards and garages. For generations, municipal politicians have been loath to permit a continued gentle densification of this area—five-storey walk-up apartment buildings remain rarities (well-organized, middle class home-owners conscious of property values are who votes in Toronto's municipal elections). Instead, the re-densification of the urban core proceeds apace. The growth has been mostly upward: older walk-ups and parking lots are being replaced by fifty-storey condominium buildings. Many people among those reciting land acknowledgements before performing arts events in Toronto are home-owners and second-home-owners. How about, instead of an Indigeneity fantasy that allows WASP Canadians the enjoyment of blood-and-belonging by proxy, we increase densification in the yellow belt and build affordable apartments so low-income and middle-income people of any ethnicity can live anywhere in the city?

The birth of Toronto through the establishment of single-family property lots did happen through colonial settlement. How about mixing it up a bit with some semblance of rent control--how about *that* kind of decolonization?

In spite the current trend toward Balkanization, polarization and racializing, we are one polity. It's bizarre that someone who has lived here only since 1999 has to keep saying this to people whose ancestors go back to Nouvelle France and the Huron of the Tabor Hill burial ground. The sooner we realize this, the faster we can begin to tackle the issues that affect all: the severely unaffordable housing in urban centres, overwork and underemployment, mental health and quality of life.

Chapter 3

HAS CANADA EVER BEEN LIBERAL, though? Was it ever clear that it should be? Was that ever the foundational dream?

And here I mean liberalism as it emerged out of the absolutist monarchies of Europe and evolved to the era of universal suffrage, universal public schooling, and innocence-presumed-until-proven-guilty. Liberalism as the idea that everybody is of equal value irrespective of caste, class, ethnicity, race, sex, religious belief, under the same set of laws created through increasingly democratic representation with a vision of a just society on the horizon – the same set of impersonal laws that trump personal and professional loyalties and familial relationships. Was this ever firmly a Canadian value, outside the writings of Janet Ajzenstat and Pierre Trudeau?

Not having experienced feudalism, civil wars, occupation, war lords, Canada's radar doesn't register that the pillars of liberalism, including the rule of law and the state's monopoly on violence, were introduced in response to sectarian might-makes-right and a life that was solitary, brutish, and short. The process of European settlement of Canada, it's been argued, is a different story of origin than a liberation from the clergy and aristocrats. Canada's founding colonies brought European neuroses to a terrain which apparently requires a radically different approach.

Part of that different approach, very much alive in Anglophone Canada today, is a keen interest in ethnicity. The country is, increasingly, I think (or has this always been a plan?) letting people take exceptions to its laws. Should you be Amish, Indigenous, or WASP parents who don't care for scientific medicine and your child dies while you're refusing them medical treatment, it's likely that you won't go to jail. If you're a First Nations person getting divorced, the question may become whether, say, Haudenosaunee laws trump Ontario family law in disputes involving your family. If you work in the Catholic public school board in Ontario, your right to decline to hire homosexuals and atheists will not be contested as no politician seeking elected office wants to tackle the system of publicly-funded religious education we've inherited from pre-Confederation days. It is quite legal today to specify in university job openings, in publishing or arts residences or art jobs the preferred ethnicity of an ideal candidate— and the astonishment at that new normal operating procedure expressed by associations like the Society for Academic Freedom and Scholarship seems like a call from another era. Conversely, Quebec's recent state laicity law, Bill 21—whose constitutionality is being contested—bans the wearing of religious symbols of any kind by workers in the public sector, potentially blocking employment of any judges, police officers, or teachers who wear Sikh turbans, kippahs, headscarves, or necklaces with a cross. (While my political instincts are close to the French secular republican one-citizenship-for-all, there is something illiberal in the will to control what somebody is wearing, even if their salary is paid by the state. I leave room for religious head coverings by chalking them up to individual eccentricity.)

This tradition of thought that sees Canada, at best, as a ramshackle stopgap in the ongoing negotiation between various irreconcilable parties and, at worst, as a noxious imperial colonizer of resources and people (genocidal even, in the language that our current prime minister accepted recently)—this tradition is doing very well. It has taken over the left and the political centre, permeated the liberal media, gained prominence in university departments of humanities and social sciences. Anybody who's applied for jobs on Canadian job boards will have noticed the rhetoric of the social justice redress in employment ads in the non-profit sector, government, social service agencies and arts organizations. The understanding that we are a country dramatically split into two races largely comes from American politics, media, and TV drama: we just cast the principal roles differently.

* * *

Not a lot of activists will have read or even heard of Prof. James Tully, but I think if we are to look for a systematizer and magus of the currently dominant progressive moral intuitions on what Canada is and what its existence is doing, this B.C-based political theorist and University of Victoria professor emeritus appears to me a perfect candidate. There's a remarkable history of liberalism-with-exceptions in Canadian thought. When I was studying political theory at Dalhousie University, the first people we read on liberal democracy were Charles Taylor and Will Kymlicka. I was thus introduced to the Quebec-inspired bilingual-binational corrective to one legal system and one unified culture, and the corrective of multiculturalism, which together, at least in arts funding, media, and shop signs, if not in laws, questioned the idea of one universal state. (The prevalence of the English language, of course, often makes the question of a deep multiculturalism moot, and I callously think it's a good thing.)

If I were to do a graduate degree in Canadian political thought today, we would be immediately reading James Tully. There are two modes of citizenship, he writes in *On Global Citizenship*. One, liberalism, is the usual kind we know about and hold as standard: it comes with nation states, modernization of society, creation and expansion of rights and responsibilities, and nation-building in the wake of decolonization. Tully calls this the Euroamerican concept of citizenship.

Liberal democracies came into being as their playing fields, nations, were forming, often brutally, and are therefore deeply polluted by this history, Tully contends. Local (and colonized) populations gave up their self-governance and local knowledge, sometimes by force, to be added to the larger liberal polity in exchange for security and enforceability of modern rights.

It follows that modern constitutionalism, Tully explains in *Strange Multiplicity*, operates in concepts of popular sovereignty which "eliminate cultural diversity as a constitutive aspect of politics" (p. 63). The people are conceived of as "a society of equal individuals in a state of nature . . . with the aim of constituting one uniform political association." The people, moreover, are taken to exist at a 'modern' level of historical development and to deliberate free of constraints of higher authority, or religious supersession. "[A] modern constitution must recognize the institutional and sociological conditions of a modern society and the type of liberty and equality that corresponds to them."

The modern theorists hold that "the conflicting jurisdictions and authorities of the ancient constitutions were the cause of wars. Accordingly, their response was that authority had to be organised and centralised by the constitution in some sovereign body: in a single person, or assembly, a system of mixed or balanced institutions, or in the undifferentiated people. Such an authority could recognize custom from time to time, as even Hobbes concedes, but custom has authority only in virtue of its recognition by the sovereign, not vice versa. In the modern theories of the sovereignty of the people, the plurality of existing ancient authorities is eliminated by construing the people as the single locus of authority and their aim is the constitution of a uniform system of government" (67).

So the modern citizenship of liberal democracies, as it has developed from the eighteenth century onward, proposes itself as universally applicable and desirable. It is a regulative ideal of citizenship, and it has been promoted in the past by explorers and missionaries with their imperial self-proclaimed rights to set up settlements and commercial ports, and in the twentieth century by international organizations like the United Nations, World Trade Organization, NATO, and assorted NGOs.

Yes, citizenship rights have continuously expanded in the history of modern citizenship, but Tully, paradoxically, holds this against liberalism. The poor, the propertyless, women, immigrants, and certain ethnicities were originally excluded from citizenship. When the illegal struggles by former non-citizens were successful, he says, they were "redescribed retrospectively as stages in the development of modern citizenship and incorporated within its framework." That these original exclusions were erased, he argues, does not make them okay. It's just another form of colonization, with the Euroamerican ideal of citizenship conquering everything in its path.

It follows, in Tully's view, that the ongoing project of Euroamerican colonization wreaks havoc wherever it goes. He has only grim news about the current state of global affairs. He talks about the hundreds of millions of malnourished around the globe, and high infant mortality rates in the developing world, and is mute on the historical decrease in world hunger and child mortality. (That those numbers exist for philosophers and social scientists to use and be monitored in the first place is thanks to supernational organizations like the detested WHO and UNICEF.)

Tully is interested in developing or positing against this background a different model of citizenship that is more focused on the local and global than the national or international, and does not see uniform laws as a straightforward value. He prioritizes difference, and differing sources of political authority, instead of a sole Hobbesian sovereign. He appreciates the "irregularity of an ancient constitution" (66).

The liberal citizenship's mantra "the rule of law, not of men" disguises the long chain of individuals and groups which have created, voted on, and are enacting those laws, says Tully, so why not open up the non-institutional, contingent aspect of law creation and practice even more? And while we're at it, let's remove sovereignty from liberalism's one supreme authority and return it to the numerous local authorities which citizens may know more closely and have ties with. He advocates for local-facing *togetherness* in which all citizens are governing and being governed in turn.

Tully notes that his two modes of citizenship have no consistent nomenclature. They have been described by different activists and thinkers in different contexts as "global citizenship from above *versus* global citizenship from below, low intensity *versus* high intensity global citizenship, representative *versus* direct, hegemonic *versus* counter-hegemonic, cosmopolitan *versus* place-based, universal *versus* multiversal. I prefer to call these two families 'modern' and 'diverse' citizenship."

While arguing for his multiversal, civic, *glocal* (sorry, reader) ideal of citizenship, Tully often gets inspired, though less specific, and more prescriptive, and occasionally veers into self-help and New Age vocabulary. While modern citizenship is egocentric, diverse citizenship is ecocentric and human-centric. Civic citizens are "'care-takers' of the goods of the dwelling places in which they live" who "listen and respond carefully to nature as a living being (Gaia) in their ecological sciences." They are culturally diverse too, Tully suggests, in an uncomplicated, cooperative manner. They prioritize communities and members *in* dwelling places and not the "liberty rights of abstract individuals". And so on.

Maybe the abstract individuals are the passenger train riders whose lives were disrupted by protests across the country in solidarity with the hereditary Wet'suwet'en in 2020 or Ottawans on week three of the city blockade by groups opposed to covid vaccine mandates? That is perhaps a crude concretization of Tully's ideas, but his ideas do appear strangely untouched by the news or most aspects of contemporary life. It's a delightfully rustic vision and it presumes, as do a lot of Canadian political intuitions, that your life includes a patch of land to call your own and take care of. It's also a vision uncomplicated by class or sexual difference: the raising of children, for example, introduces no philosophical or political complications to diverse citizenship.

And what is the dwelling of an immigrant renter in a high rise in Toronto: what is our patch of Gaia to keep an eye on? The very fact of local togetherness is in contemporary conditions likelier to produce acrimonious disputes than solidarity. The dispute over fishing quotas between the Native and non-native fishermen in Nova Scotia was very local, grassroots, and Gaia-rific. I wonder if Tully would argue today that the fishing quotas are an impersonal bureaucratic imposition? In the clash of interests between downtown Toronto park users (usually apartment dwellers and renters with no patch of land to enjoy the Gaia on) and the homeless drug users in tents in parks during the miserable covid season of 2020-21, which of the two groups speaks for the dwelling place? (The two sides should get to know each other and hang out, the *Globe and Mail's* architecture critic approvingly quoted a Montreal activist as saying at the height of the park disputes of 2020, inadvertently echoing Tully.)

Tully's vision averts the eyes from the clashing concepts of good, perhaps presuming that they would harmonize if people were just left to their own local devices.

Tully is equally vague about alternative forms of citizenship in the world that, say, Freedom House may tut-tut at. Would hereditary chieftains in the UK and Lesotho enjoy reserved places in the legislature? Would child marriage be permitted, or Mormon polygamy? What about the practice of Montenegrin daughters voluntarily giving up their share of real estate inheritance in favour of their brothers? All of those are traditional, time-tested ways of belonging to a polity. Is calling such phenomenon corruption and nepotism an imperialist, hegemonic overreach? A cold and unwarranted liberal questioning of a communal activity?

Peek inside the ruling structures of Ukraine, Russia, or Montenegro if you want to see communal practices at work. Or lift up the rug in older, wealthier democracies and notice the preferential treatment in public tenders for politically-connected corporations and individuals; the children of politicians, journalists, and artists inheriting their parents' jobs; the wildly disparate outcomes in public vs. private education, to name just a few manifestations of the communal tendency. They have always been there, even if their origins are sometimes lost in the mist of time.

Like Tully, a lot of the loudest native rights advocacy in our public discourse is 'unpindownable' about the ultimate goal. I can't quite grasp what the nation-to-nation term in Canadian political conversation actually means. If the idea is self-determination toward a legal separation and creation of a new political entity, it's a legitimate goal and it should be clearly stated. But no such luck. There's just a strong discontent with the idea of sovereignty, and with secular universalism.

* * *

I hear the phrase secular universalism and my first response is, "Yes, isn't it wonderful?"

First the individual was invented, then it was joined with others in a polity, a society, deprioritizing pedigree, guilds, ancestors, the church, and ethnicity. How is that terrible?

Tully would like us to think of a constitutionality that preserves cultural and legal plurality. There is not one national narrative, no great solidarity, but a "diversity of criss-crossing and contested narratives." People associate and belong through groups and their narratives. Constitutions are not fixed but "chains of continual intercultural negotiations" (183-4).

When approaching the conflict of fishing rights, Tully quotes a court case involving the Musqueam nation and non-Native fishers which ruled that "fishing a specific body of coastal water is constitutive of the cultural identity of the Aboriginal Musqueam" in a way that it is not for the non-Indigenous fishers, therefore the conservation quotas do not apply the same way (172).

As regards feminists, Tully has a lot of time for what in the 1990s was called cultural feminism, when several ethicists and psychologists, notably Carol Gilligan, explored the ethics of care (vs. ethics of justice) model, and whether women tend to gravitate toward it. "[F]or women to be treated fairly in discussing any constitutional issue," argues Tully, "not only issues related to their gender difference, their culturally different ways of speaking and acting need to be recognised and accommodated in the dialogue itself. One aspect of any just constitutional negotiations will be to reach agreement on which gender differences are relevant and worthy of being constitutionalised." (P. 178) These arguments about women in the public sphere have not aged well, but the identification of fishing as essential for Indigenous cultures and identity (even if it's done for commercial reasons, the same as fishing done by any other ethnicity or individual) is very much alive today. To have one set of rules for all ethnic groups would be, according to this argument, colonial and hegemonic.

For an antidote to Tully, I go to Janet Ajzenstat. This political theorist and professor emeritus of political science at McMaster University is probably the most engaging writer today on Canada as a liberal democracy. (Charles Taylor, while a beautiful thinker, is a hesitant and worried liberal democrat, of which more in another chapter.) In *The Once and Future Canadian Democracy*, Ajzenstat argues that we should scrap the divisions into left, right, and centre and look at the main division in political life as the one between liberalism and romanticism. Neither group falls neatly within its category, but generally romantics "dream of democracy as individual self-fulfilment and the expression of communal identity" and liberals "cherish freedom and justice." The recent populist turn? Not new at all: merely the most recent form of romanticism. "In Canada it's as old as Louis-Joseph Papineau, leader of the Rebellions of 1837-38. And in the Western nations generally, it's as old as the eighteenth-century philosopher Jean Jacques Rousseau. I might have chosen populism, simple democracy, or even communitarianism to describe this romantic, new-politics ideology . . . They all describe aspects of the one underlying attitude. I prefer 'romantic.' It suggests enthusiasm, yearning—impatience. In my view, impatience is central to the romantic ideology" (*The Once and Future*, p. 13).

Liberalism, too, Ajzenstat defines by its history: it started with John Locke in the seventeenth-century, an ideology of liberty, born of resistance to the absolutist monarchies of the era.

There are few people who manage to tell the political history of Canada in a way that's even remotely exciting, but Ajzenstat weds wit, poetry, and cheek. (Perhaps Kenneth McNaught's 1999 memoir *Conscience and History*, written by a wealthy socialist with P.G. Wodehouse flair, comes close.) In *The Once and Future*, Ajzenstat rolls out a lively and *parti pris* political history of Canada as the story of a *liberal* democracy, in which the unsexy things like mediation, representation, elections, parties, constitutional negotiations and the notwithstanding clause become intriguing and shiny. Part of the liberals' bad rep is that their worldview is, as Tully put it, low intensity, and whenever this charge is raised, Yeats' verses from 'The Second Coming' come to mind: "The best lack all conviction, while the worst / are full of passionate intensity."

Ajzenstat (like Richard Rorty, whom I read earlier in the post-communist Yugoslavia and Montenegro) revives what was originally exciting about the now apparently worn-out ideas that are liberal democracy, Enlightenment universalism, and liberty. While many of its early creators didn't intend to include non-Europeans, heathens, or women in its propositions, Enlightenment's promise of freedom fired up both Toussaint Louverture and the liberation struggle in Haiti, and England's Mary Wollstonecraft advocacy for women as rational, political, world-historical subjects. *Sapere aude*, dare to know, rather than believe or comply with what a proven authority says—this is Kant's answer to the question 'what is Enlightenment?' It removes the shackles from our capacity to use reason autonomously. All of us are touched by the light of reason, and all of us therefore are capable of ethical judgment, and possess dignity. (And when, in his odd minor essay, Kant added a caveat: except for those barbaric people over there, and the second sex right here, the ensuing centuries didn't take his footnotes seriously. It was too late for the genie to return to the bottle).

Mozart, Kant, Louverture, Wollstonecraft, then.

No, answers Tully, and many others, it's the East Indian Company, the

African slaves on sugar plantations in the Caribbean, and the Hudson's Bay Company.

It matters, say liberals, what kind of societies we created in our march through history. With Napoleon and after him, army recruitment democratized and was open to all, as befits this newly created solidarity called the nation. Every man is equally of a nation, therefore equally expected to fight for it, and to be rewarded by it: valour in warfare is detached from the aristocratic caste and democratized.

But the wars became more and more total, answer the romantics, involving entire populations. Nations with their capitalism gradually structured human time with mandatory schooling hours and factory and office timetables. They built prisons, and established national surveillance and controls. The nuclear family formed itself as the reproductive and survival unit, work was largely dispatched outside the home, female labour was domesticated, and women were relegated to the private sphere.

No, we invented the individual, liberals insist. We made non-conforming possible: pursue the good life, however you define it. Shall we be immodest and say we made freedom possible?

Maybe you did, but then you let the individual dissipate under technocratic and scientific scrutiny. Man may be born free but in liberal democracies he's now closely observed and his life tightly structured. Governance has spread even to human biological cells; the recent pandemic made that all too obvious. With the liberal promise of freedom comes freedom's twin sister, insecurity, which we collectively attempt to correct with our trust in scientific research, medical planning, and technocratic government. And while liberalism gave us neutrality on the question of a good life, it also let mass media, Hollywood, and social media become the ruling forces in the market of values.

The complaints of the romantics are not all unfounded: left to their own devices, humans choose coasting or indifference. Says Ajzenstat: "In their hearts, romantics want more than electoral and parliamentary change. They want a politics and society in which all say 'yes' with one strong voice. There *is* a way to reconcile individual self-realization and community. There must be!" (*The Once and Future*, 16).

For romantics, the public-private distinction is indefensible. "Romanticism isn't something you dip into in your off-hours . . . What man or woman who has experienced the greatest work of human genius, who understands the glory and despair of the human situation as Art reveals it, can then go out to debate decorous political measures under Robert's Rules of Order?" (24-5)

This takes us to a question that Richard Rorty poses in *Philosophy and Social Hope*. Young Rorty, raised by the very leftist parents, developed in his teens an obsession with wild orchids alongside his political consciousness. And esoteric flowers are useless to the social justice cause. "I was afraid that Trotsky (whose *Literature and Revolution* I had nibbled at) would not have approved of my interest in orchids." He later chose philosophy as his profession because it held the promise of uniting his two sides.

But things got complicated as Rorty read and lived some more, and the orchids were replaced by other things, equally useless to the fight for justice, like Proust's *Remembrance of Things Past*. By the time he published his second book, *Contingency, Irony, and Solidarity*, arguably his most appealing and influential work, Rorty had abandoned the hope that we can hold reality and justice in a single vision. He argued that "there is no need to weave one's personal equivalent of Trotsky and one's personal equivalent of my wild orchids together. Rather, one should try to abjure the temptation to tie in one's moral responsibilities to other people with one's relation to whatever idiosyncratic things or persons one loves with all one's heart and soul and mind . . . The two will, for some people, coincide—as they do in those lucky Christians for whom the love of God and of other human beings are inseparable, or revolutionaries who are moved by nothing save the thought of social justice. But they need not coincide, and one should not try hard to make them do so." (p. 13)

Yes, said Rorty, Proust's life and work are irrelevant to the struggle for justice, anywhere. "But that is a silly reason to despise Proust. It is as wrong-headed as Savonarola's contempt for the works of art he calls 'vanities.' Single-mindedness of this sort is the quest for purity of heart—the attempt to will one thing—gone rancid. It is the attempt to see yourself as an incarnation of something larger than yourself (the Movement, Reason, the Good, the Holy) rather than accepting your finitude . . . Your equivalent of my orchids may always seem merely weird, merely idiosyncratic, to practically everybody else." But they're both equally important: what we can agree on (the universal) on the one hand, and the idiosyncrasy, the eccentricity, of a person, on the other.

The romantics in our lives and in our shared polity will object to this. They will not care for the relegation of passions, including what Rorty called "your quaint religious faith," to the private sphere.

Did Canada, on its way to 2022, ever really dispatch religious belief to the private sphere? Or are we lingering between the American religion-infused political culture, and the British, where religion is all but gone and only appears in debates about some of the snags of multiculturalism like the blasphemy laws or Salman Rushdie's right to fictionalize Mohammad however he pleases?

Ajzenstat tells the history of Canada's piecing itself together as a proto-liberal democracy, rather unzealously and unromantically, one reform politician at a time, one provincial legislature at a time, with the exception of the Red River rebellion and Manitoba. (It's not the exception, the left romantics argue today: it's the core of the plan, no different than the unpleasant march of any other nation-state.)

It's through a bunch of liberals that Ajzenstat traces the genealogy of the concept of responsible government, which makes the executive in the colonies responsible to the representatives elected for the legislature rather than to British overlords across the ocean, even though the Britons overseas may be paying the bills. Was it Pierre Bédard in the legislative assembly of Lower Canada in 1806 who first formulated and suggested the idea of responsible government (for which he was sent to jail, it being too soon after the French revolution)? Or was it Robert Baldwin, who put it in effect? Or Lord Durham, who put it in his influential report about the troubles in the colonies? That's roughly the early genealogy.

May I pause here in order to comment what a fascinating figure Robert Baldwin (1804-1858) was, and his entire family? A depressive who accomplished everything in spite of his incapacitating melancholy, Baldwin (with Louis-Hypolite LaFontaine) laid the foundations for Canada's Anglo-Franco biculturalism in a move of democratic liberalization against the colonial Tories, he introduced an independent judiciary, opened access to the civil service, opened doors to public education, secularized the University of Toronto, and had a whole set of bills, including a bill compensating Lower Canadians for rebellion losses, passed and signed by the governor general Lord Elgin against the wishes of the British-focused Tories, who then rioted in turn. The precedent was set, and stayed. How many other Canadian and proto-Canadian politicians can brag of this kind of record? (Excepting perhaps the second premiership of Pierre Trudeau). While he is reason incarnate in public life, Baldwin's religious worship of his wife after her death took some strange forms. Shortly before he died, he left a note that he was to be buried in a coffin chained to hers, and his body incised with a scalpel in the same way hers was during the caesarean which led to an infection that she didn't survive. The note managed to find its way to the hands of some willing friends and family members who indeed opened his grave for this very purpose and did what he asked. Baldwin was a good example of the Rorty paradox, the raving mad romantic privately and a liberal under the bright lights of public life.

Various liberal democratic ideas that took hold in Canada have even longer lineage, leading back to the 1688 Revolution and earlier, writes Ajzenstat. "The idea of natural and political equality was out and about and creating trouble in politics long before English society and custom began to exhibit its effects . . . By the seventeenth century, English politics was alive with arguments for natural equality and speculation about the consequences of this teaching for politics. Thomas Hobbes and John Locke published major books on the subject, books still read and still influential, the ground of our law and politics to this day." (51) Ajzenstat traces the principle of the 'rule of law'—that no individual no matter her rank or background can escape the consequences of law or govern outside the law—to the Magna Carta issued in 1215. The state having the monopoly on violence, i.e., the existence of a police force, also has a long lineage, although it is periodically questioned in our times.

I value these liberal democratic ideals. In the part of the world where I come from, we're still working on the one-law-for-all bit. Laws are shot through with loyalties to one's family, clan, party, or colleague. In fairness, most of the world is still working out equality before the law, even Canada.

Montenegro is also struggling with the state monopoly on violence, preferring to disperse it to various groups. When you have a history of taking justice into your own hands, why would you trust something or someone else to do it? A small state, it was run by dynasties of bishop-poets who regularly took arms against occupying empires, whether Ottoman, Habsburg, or Soviet, while also contending with internecine fighting among tribes. Things were supposed to stabilize when a communist country was created, but the optimism of the first generation gave way to the cynicism of their children who started noticing that many of the officially declared rules were arbitrary, illogical, and only partially observed by the very people whose job it was to enforce them. It got worse in the 1990s when the country and all its laws fell apart. Crime became lucrative amid civil wars, and stayed lucrative in peacetime, in the newly created states. The political warring of ideological and ethnic factions is ongoing, with no Leviathan in sight (apart from the occasional EU or US functionary in a sharp suit).

* * *

Perhaps the Ajzenstat duality between the liberals and the romantics overlaps to a considerable degree with the division into universalists and identitarians today, which is another division that doesn't match the left-right divide. Those of us who see redistributive justice as more pressing will tend to gather around universalism, and those who understand justice as recognition will gravitate toward the romance of identity.

At any rate, I moved to Canada in 1999, searching for freedom: from family, ethnicity, nation, gender, poverty, an authoritarian political culture, an economy of the early accumulation of capital. I realize now that Canada's foundational principles are being questioned as well. I moved here in search of a liberal democracy, only to learn that the project is never complete, and that one can never relax and return to private life, taking various freedoms for granted. That the wild orchids often have to wait.

The first class I attended at Dalhousie, it just so happens, was "Liberalism and Democracy" in the philosophy department. Dalhousie humanities departments back then were housed in Victorian houses with creaky floors where people civilly debated pros and cons of political visions and historical interpretations, it being not a matter of life and death but a matter of discussion. I was a curious beast in the context, eventually appreciated after a manner as a product of the continental tradition of political thought and Anglo-philosophers who read bi-continentally like Richard Rorty. I landed in Nova Scotia the autumn after the summer of the NATO bombing of Serbia-Montenegro, which did stop the war in Kosovo but exponentially increased the problems in governance and left the Serb leader Slobodan Milošević to continue wielding absolute power. (Montenegro finally returned to its separate statehood with a referendum in 2006; its rulers, who had supported Serbia and Milošević and then changed course, stayed on through thirty years of electoral cycles, only losing their parliamentary majority in late 2020.) The 1990s wars left us locked out of Schengen-unified Europe which closed its doors to immigrants from the troubled east (in contrast to how German Chancellor Angela Merkel responded to the Middle Eastern refugee crisis twenty years later). Had the EU not closed its doors in the 1990s, I might be writing today in a European language, from a country on the continent, about the difficulty of belonging to *it*. Such are the vagaries of history.

The Belgrade I left had a newly pluralistic political science department where all kinds of texts were finally circulating freely. Liberal democratic thought was fighting it out with the extremely popular and ever hardening right, and the institutionalized but waning historical materialism. The fights were among the students, in conversations between students and teachers, among teachers themselves, and between teachers and the administration. It was a heady era of newly acquired freedom of thought and expression and we, the journalism and politics students who had travelled to Belgrade from afar, did our best to think and ignore how precarious our situation was amid ongoing political upheaval. Once we began interning and writing, choices had to be made: does one try to join one of the two or three liberal papers, or opt for one of the growing number of commercially viable right-wing papers. Or does one try for the government-funded outlets which are holding the pro-Milošević regime line. Could you write how you wanted to write anywhere? Only in the western liberal democracies, we were sure. The media in western liberal democracies didn't ban writers for their opinions, we were certain, and neither did their universities. We needed this to be true.

I had written my graduation thesis on Alasdair MacIntyre's critique of liberalism, since I was, as many a liberal would be, smitten by a worldview so different from mine, so compelling and self-sufficient, and so much more stable and serene and lovingly imagined than the mess of my own liberal framework. My MA thesis at Dalhousie was going to be, it transpired in two years' time, about another critic of liberal democracies: Michel Foucault. So this particular liberal of the Kant, Mill, Tocqueville and Mary Wollstonecraft kind spent a lot of time with the disciples of Aquinas and Nietzsche, the anti-liberals of the right and the anti-liberals of the left, and it seems that my time in Belgrade has forever kept me in that conversation. I kept peering at the other two over my own fence. Know thy ideological enemy and know how to respond to them, for liberal democracies and their philosophical foundations are forever tenuous.

My biggest theory crush has been, all this time, the aforementioned Rorty, an atypical liberal but very much one. (Before him, it was Karl Popper's *The Open Society and Its Enemies*, only translated after the end of communism, that provided excitement.) No, liberal democracies do not align with the fundamentals of 'human nature' as there is no such thing; but we want them because they're the societies least cruel to their weakest members, while allowing for the greatest freedom of the individual. Yes, liberal democracies produce some awful, uncaring people who *choose* not to develop their best potentials, but that is the price we must pay for the freedom to choose one's own idea of the good life, rather than accept whatever is imposed on us. Or so goes the argument.

There I was, in a quiet philosophy seminar room at Dalhousie with twenty eloquent young people and an analytical philosophy professor who tolerated, perhaps even enjoyed the eccentricity of my presentations about the body featured in philosophy and politics, about nationalism, war machines, surveillance and discipline, sexual difference, madness, when the conversation was ostensibly about procedural justice and fairness. I knew little about Canada then. I'd only seen André Melançon films for children, read a Jungian essay about Atwood's *Surfacing*, watched *North of 60* and *Les Filles de Caleb* on TV. It had only mattered to me that Canada was next to the US. (While I shed that attitude a long time ago, most Canadian-born people have not. The neighbouring country still matters more to them than their own; they are much more interested in it than in Canada.) But this calmness before difference that I witnessed in the philosophy seminar was a good sign. I realized that reasonable people, sometimes with incommensurable worldviews, can disagree and still continue the conversation. Living in liberalism means continually encountering people in the public sphere whose idea of what is good appalls or puzzles you, but whom you won't be able to legislate or force out of existence, and this is an excellent feature of the software.

When I began searching for what Canada might mean, it first took the contours of *a certain idea of fairness* as the guiding ideal. Fairness is not easily or often achieved, but it persists as an ideal. Much can be inferred about a culture based on its unwritten rules of behaviour in everyday situations.

Rebelling against orderly queuing, traffic regulations and smoking bans in cafes or public institutions gives an illusion of freedom in countries like the one that I come from. But those rebellions have comparatively vanished in Canada, an indicator perhaps of a more complex view of what freedom is, and how the threads of civic unity are more solidly woven.

I now know, after ten years of cycling in Toronto, that Toronto drivers do as the Balkan drivers do, but also that there is more outrage about it here. The media still report on the might-makes-right nature of Toronto automotive traffic toward weaker participants; the ideal of sensible traffic behaviour persists.

The week I'm writing this final chapter paragraph, I was screamed at from a car and called a fool for daring to cycle two connecting blocks on Jarvis Street. This urge to despise the physically weaker from the safety and anonymity of one's steel shield is quite possibly universal and does not disappear with the emergence of liberal democracy. What would the founders of the liberal thought have to say about a Toronto cyclist on a six-lane inner city arterial road which drivers use as a freeway between two other freeways, who has to take her life into her own hands whenever she turns onto Jarvis?

Perhaps the most serious critique of classical liberalism is the one that liberalism posits a level playing field between the bully and the weak, exactly as Toronto's traffic is set up. It presumes its free individuals are unattached to any dependent creatures, old or small. In the real world, it can be agnostic about the practices that preceded it—tribalism of the like-hiring-like, and the fact that people will almost always prefer their family and their village to everybody else, which for communitarian critics like Tully is not a bad thing. Also, violence confuses liberalism; it doesn't have a ready response to it other than the longitudinal and rational 'more education, more wealth.'

I'll be exploring all those, as well as liberalism's Jungian shadow, loneliness, in the chapters to come. I'll try to detail not only what's weakening the liberal tradition from the outside (illiberalism both right-wing and progressive) but also its inherent conundrums and snags which we should be aware of, lest they too add cracks to the liberal foundations.

Chapter 4

FREEDOM, NOT HAPPINESS, must be used as the measuring stick to assess the situation of women. Simone de Beauvoir came to this insight while writing *The Second Sex*, which documents the many ways a woman's life is predetermined and narrowed because she is born a girl. Things have gotten better since 1949 for women in most parts of the world, and are now moving asymmetrically between high-income and middle/low-income societies. One thing remains likely: bearing children, unless there's wealth, a stay-at-home partner, or a village, will take away the woman's authorship of her life for a substantial number of years. With children, her life will not be about her for a long while, if ever again. Given the unique feature of gestation available to their sex only, a lot of women decide to use it. (In many times and places motherhood is mandatory, not a choice.) It's a potentiality, in the Aristotelian sense, so why not see it to its *telos*.

Putting romantic fulfillment as one of the highest values in life leads to a similar trajectory; Beauvoir wrote about this too with a dispassionate eye. Her positing of happiness and freedom as two ends that do not overlap is not by accident.

In Doris Lessing's *The Golden Notebook*, we read of the *free women*, probably an equal part ironic and aspirational description that the narrator and her friends give to themselves. They are de Beauvoir's offspring, too. While Anna is conscious of what needs to be done, in personal and political life, to free herself, she falls apart; a vicious love affair with a man engulfs her life to the point of madness. Lessing was too much a truth teller to ignore the patterns women fall into and can't easily abandon, even if they are fully aware of how noxious those patterns can be.

The crest of this wave of new feminist fiction in anglophone publishing was just around the corner. Young Margaret Drabble wrote about young women who leave relationships and pursue non-romantic goals such as a life in the arts. Margaret Atwood, Angela Carter, A.S. Byatt, and many more, were changing the available narratives. Many were mothers too, unlike most of the previous generations of women writers in English, and intent on showing that the two callings can co-exist. Recent years have seen an excellent amount of honest writing, by mothers, about mothering and its contradictory impulses, its hardship, loneliness, narcissism. As Donald Winnicott said a long time ago, mothers must keep the integrity of their own selves and let down the child gently; the child must learn that it cannot own the mother and that it will survive the relinquishing of control. Literary mothers are finally letting the offspring down for the most part gently by telling the truth.

Yet the materiality of childrearing, and the sociology of it, is inexorable. Women still do the vast majority of it, and even in lesbian couples there is a primary caregiver (although parenting is somewhat more equally distributed). Motherhood still takes over women's lives and decentres them in their own stories. A marriage and a child is a supporting role waiting to happen. In this, Beauvoir's instincts proved sharp.

Don't children, however, provide a tremendous substitute to the answer of life's purpose? The substitute performs so well that it works as the thing itself, as a genuine answer to the question of meaning. Those of my cohort who have children are going through the milestones with them, and reliving and thinking through their own childhood and parents. A forty-seven-year-old who is not married, not a parent, and a freelancer not attached to a company by full-time employment will have to take a lot of decisions every week, anew and anew, some deadly trivial and others more demanding, like *what is my life about this Thursday? Next Wednesday?* When there's no writing work, and no social obligations, the empty hours echo with questions. All that is amplified for an immigrant without children and marriage to root them to a new country and continuously bring new people and activities.

I could have married, had children, I could have had a life, says Chantal Akerman in more than one place in her memoir, *My Mother Laughs*, which came out in English after the filmmaker took her own life (not long after her mother's death). I understand why those thoughts spring up after a mother's death particularly. I cannot explain why, but the thoughts of the pointlessness of an unpartnered, childless life assailed me for years after my mother's death. We have leapt in gigantic steps across generations, from her mother, who was a barely literate widow of a partisan killed in the resistance against the occupation in the Second World War; to herself, managing to complete a vocational college while raising children and working in a kindergarten; to me, with an MA in political theory who is writing in the globally dominant language. A lot of that leaping was due to free public schooling in communist Yugoslavia from the nursery to the post-graduate level, and some of it to the end of communism and the early days of internet-era globalization (the internet itself being a government-funded communication channel initially).

Wherever and whenever they are given a choice and a minimum of prosperity and education, women choose to have fewer or no children. I so wanted to escape the family life modes available to me that I put an ocean between me and everybody I knew. Had I stayed in Montenegro, by now I would have been a middle-aged mother of two. Happier? Unhappier? Arguably less free. What would have been my politics? Would I have relented in the face of the regime of thirty years and worked within the regime-run institutions and media, as most in Montenegro had to do? Or stayed independent but on the margins? This is how writers divided in Montenegro in the last three decades.

* * *

Couples will keep having babies, or adopting them, no matter the societal upheavals. What I see coming to its end in large Canadian cities (and elsewhere in the G7), and what I miss very much, is the already quaint practice of friendship. There used to be a category of people we carved out a recurring chunk of time for, even though we did not date them, they were not family, or someone who could further our careers. A disinterested relationship where both sides give increasingly and correspondingly in a virtuous circle of intellectual, emotional, ethical investment. Aristotle knew that asymmetrical friendships are not proper friendships, and that there is a justness to friendship—it can be a field where we take our virtues (of, say, bravery, truthfulness) for a walk. There is a long canon of friendship in western philosophy and literature from Aristotle through Cicero, Montaigne, Johnson and Boswell, not to mention military dyads of brothers in arms from the Iliad through to twentieth-century wars.

Friendship in the canon has been heavily male, but the latter part of the twentieth century has brought changes, particularly in literature and other narrative arts like film and television, which imagine friendship between women as Aristotle saw friendship between men: as a project, as something more than a sum of its parts, as a polygon for the virtue ethics, politics, or creativity. (As Alasdair MacIntyre points out in *After Virtue* on the topic of Jane Austen, heterosexual marriage was the one field of virtue reliably available to women.) There are writers today who assure me that friendship between women is possible despite the unfavourable conditions for it at many a historic turn. They have imagined it, they have seen it, and they are testifying. Some elite cultural movements have grown out of and back into a network of personal friendships (the Bloomsbury circle, for example). Political movements often rely on an underpinning structure of friendship among primary actors (the memoirs of the Czech Velvet Revolution show that this was the case). Some American feminists have described the rise of the second feminist wave as an expanding possibility of friendship between women. Alice Echols, Ann Snitow and Rachel Blau DuPlessis documented the networks of New York radical feminists, and in fiction, the recent HBO series *Mrs America*, about the collaborative work of Betty Friedan, Gloria Steinem, Bella Abzug, and many others, shows women who are extremely serious about their political purpose and about their friendships, the two going hand in hand. The revival of feminist activism in the UK in the last five years through grassroots organizations like Women's Place UK, Fair Play for Women, the journal *The Radical Notion*, Helen Lewis's era at the *New Statesman* which nurtured several feminist writers, the 'Woman: Adult Human Female' billboard project and much else—all was made possible, as many women attest themselves, because it was easy to get together in a pub on short notice (good train connections, smaller distances). Social media played a part, YouTube and Twitter in particular, but the real-life ease of getting together was decisive. You have to be willing to show up, *and* it should not be a pain or expensive to show up.

Reading about female friendships — in the works of Elena Ferrante, Zadie Smith, Victoria Wood, Margaret Drabble — is life-giving. I have seen some enduring female friendships in the wild, but I have not experienced one since grade school. Fewer women available for friendship have been coming into my life since then, and many more men, to this day. I always have multiple semi-friendships with men on the go, some long distance which have come out of opera and literature Twitter, and fewer that are local, usually by political and aesthetic affinities. They are not deep friendships. They are, in Aristotelian taxonomy, friendships of pleasure/leisure and utility, not of virtue. There is a Viber friend in Montenegro, a writer I've known since the late nineties, who resolutely only wants to discuss ideas with me; whenever I bring actual, material life into the conversation, he embarrassedly looks away.

With women I meet, the differences between us often appear unbridgeable. No owner can be friends with a renter in Toronto today, I muse after I delete yet another contact, one I haven't typed in a couple of years, from my phone. Mothers can't really understand the childless. Middle-class university lecturers cannot really understand the freelance precariat. And the married, including the lesbian married, can never have a deep friendship with an unpartnered woman. There is a certain messiness in rapports with men that makes these differences somehow paler, contextually negotiable, perhaps because my recent friendships with men have been less profound. Perhaps women want all or nothing, and want their female friends to be exactly like them. I have no good explanation.

Sex difference aside, friendship in general, as an institution, as a practice, is on the way out. I have only lived in Toronto in the last fifteen years but we are no different; international data bears my intuitions out. Noreena Hertz's 2020 book *The Lonely Century* assembles all the latest research on loneliness, which is increasing globally, not just in high-income countries. Surveys in nations and cities around the world reveal that people who feel lonely range from one in five to one in two. Hertz looks at the economic, technological and philosophical causes of the increasing loneliness and argues that it's the neoliberalism of the 1980s on, and the 2008 economic crash and subsequent austerity which have intensified work hours, increased income inequalities, and sped up the atomization in the economies of the Anglosphere. Social media and screen mediation are changing person-to-person interaction capacity. And covid lockdowns have exacerbated the weariness of being in the same space with another human, and wrecked business models which rely on physical presence and people leaving their homes to achieve a goal. Hertz argues that a lonely, atomized citizen is especially easy prey for populist anti-expert politics and conspiracy theories. This is of course no new idea: the early psychologists of the crowd, including Gustave Le Bon, Elias Canetti, and Freud, wrote about the embrace of the crowd as a cure for the aches of loneliness and confusion. Theorists of nationalism built on it.

Toronto has had its own challenges and is becoming less liveable by the day. About half of all Torontonians live in apartments, but we have to squeeze into the 5 percent of the land where intensification is allowed. Much of Toronto (200 square km) and Canada remain home-owning: about 60 percent of Canadians live in a single detached, semi-detached, or row house. Berlin, a city to which many Canadian artists have moved in the last twenty years, recently introduced a five-year freeze on rents, while Toronto's continue to rise. It took a pandemic to edge the rental vacancy rates in Toronto from under 1 percent to above 2 percent, which quickly corrected itself downward as the pandemic begin to ebb. There are 2,500 condo corporations in Toronto, whereas built rentals remain scarce and, if created at all, are geared toward high earners. Yet most condominiums

— tiny, overpriced, balcony-less, dizzyingly high, made out of glass walls — get sold before construction is complete. Some go to investors, some to owners who rent them remotely. Perhaps the absentee-owner tax in Toronto will budge the rental availability? Few people who earn $50,000 and under, therefore few people who work in arts and culture, can buy a condominium in Toronto, the cheaper of the two homeownership options. By some reports, already in 2018, only the low six-figure income qualifies for a mortgage.

Downtown east, the Upper Jarvis area, where I've rented since 2017, is in that 5 percent of city land where intensification reigns. The street faces of Yonge, Charles, upper Sherbourne, Church, Carlton, Shuter, Dundas East, River, and King East have changed radically since I first tried to write about them in my fiction a decade ago, becoming tower-filled wind tunnels. In one of the chapters in my first novel, two characters walk around Toronto discussing the few examples of Georgian architecture surviving in the city. Even more are gone now. The stretch of facades near the King Edward Hotel is taken down behind condominium and office complex scaffolding. Three wee homes on Shuter now serve as a façadism ornament to the condominium tower in the back. The four red brick houses on lower Church Street that also appear in the novel are being surrounded and engulfed, and whenever I pass by I wonder how much longer they'll be there.

Meanwhile, how are condo architectural styles changing the city's profile? Most of them look alike. The tallest usually come in some shape of Jenga or Lego construction, made of glass components; it's cheaper to build in glass than in brick. Surely nobody believes these are built for posterity? How many decades can an all-glass fifty-storey last? We have given up on creating things to last centuries. No centuries can be imagined. Perhaps condo buildings get slated for demolition due to psychological obsoleteness before the glass begins to fall from them?

One of the earliest things that life in Canada has taught me is that nothing lasts. Nothing is built to last. Buildings, clearly, but more importantly homes, friendships, marriages, jobs, careers. Entire cultures. City streets. There is now a cannabis store every three doors on Queen Street West; a multi-national fast food or coffee chain, or a Weston family-owned outlet, on all the most attractive downtown streets. And after the covid crisis this development is likely to continue.

Conditions such as economic precarity, unaffordable city living, continuous disruption and replacement of things and, as Hertz and many others correctly diagnosed, self-interest as the supreme value, undermine the institution of friendship. Even the title of Robert Putnam's classic study of the great American withdrawal from civic and volunteer activities, *Bowling Alone*, sounds quaint today. *Who plays anything outside the home? How peculiar.* And yet amateur sports must be a good way to find friends. Aleksandar Hemon writes in *The Book of My Lives* (2013) that local amateur chess and soccer groups in Chicago served as early entry points into the US for his integrated life there. He would just show up and join whatever game was happening whenever another player was needed. Later, he got married. Twice. For those who have emigrated to a distant country as adults *sans* family it will be additionally hard to make stable friendships where they live. My own informal polling of the people I know who have emigrated as adults reveals that it is a hard nut to crack, and that if there are to be any close friends, they, too, will be immigrants. The friendships of youth are easily made as we both pass through the same set of milestones, jump the same obstacles, or endure the same life processes shoulder to shoulder or in full view of each other. Already graduate school is too late, as we are each set on our own paths. A two-university 2007 study of friendship maintenance through cell phone conversation time and frequency concluded that we start shedding friends at about the age of twenty-five. Other studies that have looked at the friendship and age interplay from other angles tend to confirm the thinning out hypothesis.

In what must be another sign of us reaching the critical mass of solitariness, it's finally become acceptable to write publicly about one's friendlessness. "It didn't take lockdown to make me realise that I don't really have any friends, but it probably helped," writes British journalist and editor Stig Abell in May 2020. "I don't say this in a self-pitying way; I have always operated under the belief that life splits into three areas—work, family, friends—and it is possible to devote attention properly to just two of them. I have always chosen the first two." A couple of months later, Claire Bushey, a Chicago-based *Financial Times* correspondent: "When you're lonely, lockdown doesn't end. Rather horribly, the isolation the pandemic has imposed this year is not that different from my normal life. I live alone, I work alone, I'm hundreds of miles from my family. There's no real difference between not making plans (because of a virus) and not having plans (because last-minute cancellation is now socially acceptable). All of which feels shameful—these admissions leave me frantic to declare that I am hilarious, smart and quite fun to have a drink with." And Josh Glancy, the Washington Bureau chief for London's *The Sunday Times*: "It's well established that our real-life social networks are shrinking, but what really troubles me is the stat from the 2019 Sainsbury's Living Well Index survey that showed nearly half of Brits spend time with friends once a month or less. For many of us friendship is a second-tier activity."

Friendship is on its way out in anglophonia, Canada included. Numerous human practices exist for a limited period only. Take the playing of music at home. Amateur musicianship came with a middle-class home for more than a century. Between the early Romantic period of the German Lieder to the Cole Porter era, a healthy market for sheet music was a thing that existed, and a source of income for songwriters.

Today in Canada, it's rather hard to find someone who will accept a free piano. We also read fewer books, fiction especially; Canadian fiction, most especially. It seems that novel reading, too, is on its way out.

Why does it matter if we become a people who don't read and can't maintain friendships? Who live in cities divided into one class living a detached single-family pastoral and another class sardined into thirty-storey towers? Or that 85 percent of us in the workforce do not feel engaged in our jobs? Not to mention the insatiable demand for mood-altering drugs, or the readiness to put our eldest and frailest family members away and out of sight in purpose-built institutions (many of them for-profit). Is this to lead a good life? Are our lives good? We each have only one and precious. We should give it some thought. Even though my beloved liberalism would rather look away when asked about it.

Chapter 5

W E SELF-CREATE, but up to a point. Freedom to make authentic choices, to become — in the words of Alexander Nehamas — who we are, takes place against a given set of horizons. As Charles Taylor writes in The Ethics of Authenticity: "Only if I exist in a world in which history, or the demands of nature, or the needs of my fellow human beings, or the duties of citizenship, or the call of God, or something else of this order *matters* crucially, can I define an identity for myself that is not trivial. Authenticity is not the enemy of demands that emanate from beyond the self; it supposes such demands."

Freedom to go away and put an ocean between oneself and one's parents is dandy, but the question will inevitably emerge, as it did for me in middle age: OK, and then you will do what with the unprecedented freedom from the parental gaze? Freedom is a beginning of something, a tool for something.

Some of us of European origin are very careful with the word *community*. In Canada, it means anything from a group of strangers living on the same block to an entire town or a line of work. The arts *community*. The science *community*. On the continent that remembers its ethno-nationalism (in many regions still practices it) and has extensive records of its pre-modern, pre-liberal times of the divine right of kings and the Great Chain of Being, we talk cautiously about *Gemeinschaft*. The community, the *Gemeinschaft*, presumes informal connections between people, the economy of gift and not one of monetary exchange, solidarity rather than competition: a loving (like a family) or nasty (like the village in Michael Haneke's film *The White Ribbon*) environment, often both at the same time to different people. The ideal type of its opposite, the *Gesellschaft*, as sociologists Ferdinand Tönnies and Max Weber described it, is an impersonal society where the rules are general, self-interest is pursued and unemotional cooperation prevails. There is a mix of the two types, in various ratios, in all states, regions and cities.

There is a kind of loss of freedom in our societies, writes Charles Taylor, which Alexis de Tocqueville saw already in the 1830s, after his visit to the US. "A society in which people end up as the kind of individuals who are 'enclosed in their own hearts' is one where few will want to participate actively in self-government. They will prefer to stay at home and enjoy the satisfactions of private life, as long as the government of the day produces the means to these satisfactions and distributes them widely." (The Ethics of Authenticity, p. 9) The danger is not so much a despotic control, as a fragmentation: people seeing themselves, atomistically, as "less and less bound to their fellow citizens in common projects and allegiances. They may indeed feel linked in common projects with some others, but these come more to be partial groupings rather than the whole society." (113) An ethnic minority, a religion or ideology, or some special-interest cause – that will be an easy substitute. "[T]he idea that the majority of people might frame and carry through a common project comes to seem utopian and naïve" and Taylor here means on the level of the state, or multi-state or, as in the case of ecological causes, the planet. With this lack of identification with the polity as a community, people will begin to see it purely instrumentally.

Some liberal democrats see nothing wrong with this. My ethical horizon ends with my family, or myself; a city or a nation is the payroll taxes and the flat tax that is the GST, the utilities bill to be paid each month, the vehicle license renewal and the traffic regulations, the phone services 911 and 311. Others add to this their own ethnic group. Canadian multiculturalism, an idea we are proud of, in fact functions as widespread mutual indifference. Once an immigrant lands, it's up to her to make herself part of the Canadian citizenship. If she comes from a large ethnic group, say from China, Hong Kong, India, the Caribbean, Ukraine? All the better: pre-existing associations that her ethnic group has formed will receive her and integrate her into the support networks. Come from a small ethnic group? Do not want to belong to a diaspora community? She will be on her own. Canada will not offer a workable national narrative or history. The all-Canadian cultural quiddity is scarce. There are some stories available, but we're more likely to inherit those of our own ethnic groups as a permanently temporary measure. Meanwhile, let's check out what's on US cable channels and streaming services?

Until I came across Robert Putnam's research into the effects of ethnic diversity on civic engagement, the 2007 book "E Pluribus Unum: Diversity and Community in the Twenty-First Century," I refused to believe my own experience. Surely, we are all befriending and dating people of all other ethnicities, and working with people of all other ethnicities and working on joint civic or national projects with people of other ethnicities? It's probably just me who's not witnessing this in her own life, I thought. But in large American cities, people tend to hunker down among their own, pull away from broader civic engagement. Putnam's research finds this happening even as the possibility of associating with a great number of different people rises. The civic trust, in other words, the willingness to cooperate with different people to solve shared problems, decreases as diversity increases.

Sociologists have taken up the challenge of testing the Putnam thesis around the globe, in different ways and among different ethnic groups. Many confirm the findings, albeit in a limited number of contexts. A twenty-year study of nineteen western democracies found that "immigration can have a negative effect on social trust, organizational membership, and political engagement, but that institutional arrangements shape this relationship in systematic ways. In more economically equal societies . . . the negative effects of immigration on trust and engagement are mitigated" (Kesler and Bloemrad, 2010).

Another study (Stolle, Soroka, Johnston, 2008) looking at the US and Canada confirms the short-term negative effect of neighborhood diversity on white majorities across the two countries, but also finds that the effects can be mediated by social ties: "individuals who regularly talk with their neighbours are less influenced by the racial and ethnic character of their surroundings than people who lack such social interaction."

A study of forty-four developed countries (Anderson and Paskeviciute, 2006) confirms that "ethnic and linguistic diversity affects citizenship behaviour, measured by cognitive and interpersonal engagement about politics, membership in voluntary associations, and interpersonal trust," but in mixed ways on the individual level. "The only dependent variable on which heterogeneity has a consistently negative influence is trust." And "while ethnic heterogeneity decreases levels of trust in established democracies, the dimension of heterogeneity that diminishes trust in less democratic countries is language." Heterogenenity in less democratic countries can have mobilizing and politicizing results, therefore increasing engagement.

A comparative study of neighbourhood diversity and social capital in the US and Britain (Fieldhouse and Cutts, 2010) found that in both countries the white majority neighbourhood norms seem to be negatively related to diversity, but the two countries differ in the way minorities respond to diversity. "Other things being equal, community participation among British minorities is lower than expected in diverse areas."

My own life experience confirms that linguistic and ethnic diversity contributes to mistrust. I can only hope that it is a relatively short-term tendency, not a lost cause, and that the second generation of immigrants are much more willing to intermarry and mix up. According to Statistics Canada reports, under 5 percent of all Canadian couples are mixed union, that is, 'visible minority' with Caucasian, or visible minority with a different visible minority. But Canadian-born visible minorities have a higher proportion of mixed unions than their foreign-born counterparts.

The vast majority of people do not have a universal outlook or a catholic preference: they grow their world one person or one occasion or one foreign TV show at a time, if they are willing. Immigrants know this. Users of dating apps, where ethnic preferences are clearly spelled out as nowhere else in the society, know this too. I would accept the criticism that it is unreasonable to expect that every citizen of the multi-ethnic mosh pit that is Toronto should express equal interest in all (to them) foreign cultures. Good public schooling is there to make the mixing possible, but a lot of people prefer schools that are not in the commons but separate in some way, whether along ethnic, religious, or prosperity lines.

While first-generation children are not a lost cause, the zero generation, their parents, almost certainly are. It is easier to gravitate towards your own rather than start from scratch on everything and cross boundaries between people. Sometimes immigrant Canadians who work in settlement agencies designed particularly to ease integration in Canada will choose to group services and locations along ethnic lines. I worked for a couple of years as an administrative hand at an agency that had a downtown division mostly run by the Chinese, and it serviced predominantly Chinese Torontonians. A north city location was run by Iranians, and served Iranians. (How was it being the lowest-rank one-year contract worker in an office where the mid-level and management people who hired you conversed with each other in Cantonese, a language you can't speak? Not easy. On the other hand, they did hire me and let me escape the roiling hell that is Ontario Works social assistance, which covered only half of my rent on a bachelor apartment in a converted flower shop in the Junction.)

Why should a Montenegrin live in Toronto? A Serb in Switzerland? A Croat in Australia? These wealthy countries are not renewing demographically at a pace necessary to maintain the current level of prosperity, and certainly need immigration. And people who live in countries with eventful histories will sometimes want a break from the political upheaval and low-income cycle. The economy of it is understandable. But will the emigrants be happier, more fulfilled, live more meaningful lives? Debatable. There is some research, not a great deal of it, on the happiness of leavers vs. stayers. One study found differences that depended on the country of origin: the leavers from Russia and Turkey to western Europe described themselves as happier than leavers from Poland.

As mentioned earlier, I've mostly encountered immigrants to Canada whose friends or partners are other immigrants, either of their own or other countries of origin. I've known entire families not quite belonging if they come from a small ethnic group (say, Bosnian) without pre-existing support systems in Canada, and especially if the children are in their late teens or older at the time of transfer. Are these questions too impolite for Canadian immigration researchers to tackle: what ethnicity are your friends, do you have any to begin with, does your life here make sense to you? I would love to read papers on these topics. Many exist on economic integration and employment. Is that all that's important?

Early in the pandemic lockdown, (April 2020), John Gray published an essay in the New Statesman about all of us on the planet retreating from peak globalization, returning to a more local, national, and environmentally-aware existence. "An economic system that relied on worldwide production and long supply chains is morphing into one that will be less interconnected. A way of life driven by unceasing mobility is shuddering to a stop." Predictions like these seem to have already been disproved as I write this chapter, in the early spring of 2021. Self-sufficiency in producing personal protective equipment, or vaccines, seems like an abandoned priority now. But Gray's pessimism about human instincts is lucid. "It is only by recognising the frailties of liberal societies that their most essential values can be preserved," he writes. "Along with fairness they include individual liberty which as well as being worthwhile in itself, is a necessary check on government. But those who believe personal autonomy is the innermost human need betray an ignorance of psychology, not least their own. For practically everyone, security and belonging are as important, often more so. Liberalism was, in effect, a systematic denial of this fact." But Charles Taylor has already been through that narrow passage and is more optimistic. Humans will continue to be meaning-making animals, but imposed or unreflectively inherited meaning systems are not the solution to fall back on. It is, metaphysically speaking, too late. In the words of Janet Ajzenstat, "Charles Taylor dabbles [in romanticism]. He cannot believe liberal democracy is sufficient for human flourishing and yet he continues to admire it. Thus, he supports the building of a

Québécois way of life to distinguish the citizens of Quebec from other populations on the North American continent but hopes at the same time that the Quebec will *not* differ from other jurisdictions in its adherence to broad principles of liberal-democratic justice."

I have been wondering what Canadian culture is for two decades now, particularly in recent years, as the Americanization of our psyche proceeds at a confident clip. Why should we need a national culture together with a country, and is Canada not a case of one without the other? There is no country without a culture, but sometimes that culture is a culture of another nation, neighbouring or not. I remember how liberating it felt to adopt Americanisms to piss off the ethno-nationalists in the Balkans. It was also something that set you apart from the generation of your parents. But from Canada in 2021, looking back at the year of global defund-the-police protests against *American* police brutality, one realizes how deeply American culture permeates every nation thanks to the internet. It's to the point where countries desire to have American problems because there are already extensive vocabularies, images, and analyses available on those problems in English, which makes them shareable and readable around the world. American culture wars taking place on the internet become everybody's culture wars. As Helen Lewis writes in *The Atlantic* about the uptick in Britain's Americanization in 2020, "Sharing the internet with America is like sharing your living room with a rhinoceros. It's huge, it's right there, and whatever it's doing now, you sure as hell know about it." The entire world has become Canada, although we called it sleeping next to an elephant, not a rhino.

There are many ways in which we are gutting our national culture by own conscious choice. It used to be possible to make a half living or full living as an arts and culture writer in Canada. (I suspect professional dancers, actors, and musicians would attest that real income from the arts in Canada has fluctuated radically over the last sixty years and that some disciplines have seen a steady decline in monetization. I wonder if the Canada Council might take a minute away from their new decolonization mission and consider a longitudinal study of artists income and quality of life?)

Now that neither the four dailies in Toronto nor the CBC nor many of the extremely few remaining magazine editors have much interest in arts and books, that kind of life is gone. The same internet onslaught on journalism business has taken place in the UK and the US as well, but the broadsheets there maintain their arts coverage, and the BBC has stayed steady on the beat. It's not that Canadians don't need culture in their lives; it's that media managers are deciding for them that they don't, and abandoning the sections to the dwindling spiral of less coverage, less investment in talent, and less traffic, which leads to less coverage, and so on.

The summer of 2020 also saw a feverish ideologization of arts criticism, arts funding bodies in Canada, art organizations, and artists themselves. It is quite possible that the entire art funding system is about to radically change. If the Canada Council and provincial and municipal art councils prioritize art that promotes the values of respect, safety, representation, positive role-modeling, equality, fixing injustices, cultural appropriateness, 'decolonization' and indigenization — and, so beloved by the Canada Council, the digital initiatives—we will soon find ourselves in a different culture having very different conversations. No pre-existing art criticism will be around to raise pesky questions. Art will not be a miraculous connection between a unique, inimitable individual that is its creator, and a unique, inimitable individual that is its reader, viewer or listener. It will be about groups. It will home us, not send us on our way. It will be all Trotsky, no wild orchids.

For my own needs, I have been creating a list of the Canadian cultural creations that have meant a great deal to me, that have elucidated the country and drawn it close. I am fighting off the feeling that the making of that list has been an exercise in archaeology.

Chapter 6

My list, subjective, and susceptible to revision and addenda

FILM

La Guerre des tuques (1984), directed by André Melançon

Bach et Bottine (1986), André Melançon

Niagara Fools (1956), a Woody Woodpecker cartoon

Continental, un film sans fusil (2007), Stéphan Lafleur

Le Déclin de l'empire américain (1986), Denys Arcand

L'Âge des ténèbres (2007), Denys Arcand

Les Amours imaginaires (2010), Xavier Dolan

Chloe (2009), Atom Egoyan

Stories We Tell (2012), Sarah Polley

Take This Waltz (2011), Sarah Polley

Lost Song (2008), Rodrigue Jean

Ceux qui font les révolutions à moitié n'ont fait que se creuser un tombeau
(2016), Mathieu Denis, Simon Lavoie

Guibord s'en va-t-en guerre (2015), Philippe Falardeau

La Moitié gauche du frigo (2000), Philippe Falardeau

Frozen River (2008), Courtney Hunt

This Beautiful City (2007), Ed Gass-Donnelly

White Palms (Hungarian original: Fehér tenyér, 2006), Szabolcs Hajdu

Mouthpiece (2018), Patricia Rozema

Master and Commander: The Far Side of the World (2003), Peter Weir

Why Women Run (documentary, 1999), Meredith Ralston

Forbidden Love (doc., 1992), Lynne Fernie & Aerlyn Weissman

Rain, Drizzle, and Fog (doc., 1998), Rosemary House

The Angry Inuk (doc., 2016), Alethea Arnaquq-Baril

Club Native (doc., 2008), Tracey Deer

TV

Slings & Arrows (series, 2003-2006)

My 90-Year-Old Roommate (online series, 2016)

The Newsroom (series, 1996-2005)

Letterkenny (series, 2016-)

North of 60 (series, 1992-1997)

L'été . . . c'est péché (live daytime show, 2001-2004)

Tout le monde en parle (live evening talk show, 2004-)

BOOKS: FICTION

Douglas Glover: Elle (2003)

Helen Weinzweig: Basic Black with Pearls (1980)

Greg Kearney: Mommy Daddy Baby (2004)

Madeleine Thien: Simple Recipes (2001)

Dionne Brand: Theory (2018); Love Enough (2014)

Margaret Atwood: Surfacing (1972); Cat's Eye (1988)

Martha Baillie: The Incident Report (2009)

Barry Webster: The Sound of All Flesh (2005)

Zsuzsi Gartner: Better Living Through Plastic Explosives (2011)

Misha Glouberman, Sheila Heti: The Chairs Are Where the People Go
(2011)

Sheila Heti: How Should a Person Be? (2010)

Alexandra Oliver: Let the Empire Down (2016); Meeting the Tormentors
in Safeway (2013)

Seth: Clyde Fans (2019)

Emily Schultz: Heaven is Small (2009)

Russell Smith: Muriella Pent (2005)

Chester Brown: Louis Riel (2003)

BOOKS: NON-FICTION

Nick Mount: Arrival (2017)

Margaret Atwood: Survival (1972)

Taras Grescoe: Sacré Blues (2000)

George Grant: Lament for a Nation (1965)

Katherine Fierlbeck: Political Thought in Canada (2006)

Janet Ajzenstat: The Once and Future Canadian Democracy (2003)

Kenneth McNaught: Conscience and History: A Memoir (1999)

Adam Bunch: The Toronto Book of the Dead (2017)

Carl Wilson: Celine Dion's Let's Talk About Love: A Journey to the End
of Taste (2007)

Bob Gilmour: Claude Vivier: A Composer's Life (2014)

Alex Good: Revolutions: Essays on Contemporary Canadian Fiction (2017)

Any English-French dictionary of *faux amis*

Tim Clayton, Sheila O'Connell: Bonaparte and the British: Prints and
  Propaganda in the Age of Napoleon (2015)

Daša Drndić: Umiranje u Torontu (1997)

THEATRE & OPERA & DANCE

Diane Flacks: Unholy (2019)

Evalyn Parry, Laakkuluk Williamson Bathory, Erin Brubacher, Elysha
  Poirier with Cris Derksen: Kiinalik, These Sharp Tools (2018)

Ex Machina / Robert Lepage: Lipsynch (2008)

Michael Healey: The Drawer Boy (1999); Proud (2012)

Crystal Pite, Jonathon Young: Betroffenheit (2015)

Harry Somers, Mavor Moore: Louis Riel (1967)

Christopher House, Jordan Tannahill: Marienbad (2016)

Linda Griffiths: Maggie and Pierre (1980)

Ana Sokolović: Svadba (2011); dawn always begins in the bones (2017)

Brian Current: Airline Icarus (2015)

POP & FOLK

Gilles Vigneault

Arcade Fire

Stan Rodgers

Gordon Lightfoot

Diane Dufresne

Chapter 7

I HAVE BEEN TRYING TO belong to Canada in ways apart from writing, my one inroad into it, but the attempts have met with negligible success. I would have liked a belonging in flesh, an obligation, a place where I am expected. I complained once to a friend who was an ordained minister that if I disappeared at that very moment nobody would notice. She refused to partake in my self-pity and said I needed to make myself indispensable by giving of myself. "Why don't you give yourself over to something, help other people?" she asked. Although that friendship did not survive in the long run, either, the advice is good and I took it seriously.

The many jobs I've held alongside writing came with numerous work-friendships, none of which survived the end of the work contract. It was similar with volunteering. I distributed meals-on-bike-wheels in west Toronto one season, but then winter came and we car-less were put on pause. By the next spring, the volunteer coordinator had moved on to another organization and we lost touch.

I then applied to volunteer at an adult literacy organization in Parkdale. The first step was to attend a two-day *anti-oppression training* session for which I had to take a Friday off from work. I could volunteer at a big museum, like the ROM or the Gardiner! A volunteer training session revealed the amount of unpaid labour that these organizations with huge budgets, both in public funding and sponsorships, have no qualms taking. All the public-facing positions are unpaid: receptionists, ticket sales, gift shop attendant, museum guide. I decided I did not want to partake in an exploitative fandom economy. Volunteer ushers at the Soulpepper theatre had a better deal; direct supervision by a paid front-of-house staffer, about thirty minutes altogether of active work, and a reserved back seat to watch the plays. (This is how I saw Tom Stoppard's The Real Thing with Megan Fallows and Albert Schultz several times in the impecunious mid-oughts.) The ushering was meant to last a short while. After a season, I began earning enough to pay for all of my entertainment without having to volunteer for it.

Perhaps I could volunteer with the group that picks fruit from people's backyards and donates one third to the food banks, one third to the pickers, and the final third to the tree owner? That was pleasant if chaotic, until I had to move across town, to the east end, outside the program's catchment area. And then last year I joined a kid mentorship program. The training was intense, and after it: the waitlist. Those who owned cars were more useful as they could drive to the areas where the need for mentors was greatest, and they would be matched faster. The rest of us relying on public transit would have to wait.

I eventually did mentor a six-year-old at an after school program for a summer. The adorable but distracted girl, imagination running wild, began to trust me after we'd made drawings, built paper dresses, painted bird houses, played charades, read a few Dr Seuss picture books. Finally, the wild inventions petered out in conversation. Our chats settled and became more focused. We had a day trip to Fort York on a Canada Day weekend and in one of our streetcar journeys an older man who struck up a conversation with her presumed I was her mother. Before I could correct him, our stop arrived. I was given a glimpse of a pleasure reserved for parents only: proudly listening to your little one engage in a competent conversation with a stranger on the streetcar. In the autumn, however, her parents moved to a house across town, the summer after school mentorship program ended, her mother got busy, and we lost touch. Nothing lasts, nothing is built to last.

After I finish the work on this book, if the lockdowns subside, I intend, Sisyphus-like, to return to the search for meaningful volunteering engagement. Or give up for good? I often wonder what will happen when I lose my current admin job of six years in a co-op building, which has paid my bills when the writing gigs were down, or payments late. Am I going to be looking for more precarious jobs into my fifties and sixties and further, forever reformatting resumes, writing mandatorily cheerful cover letters into my old age? And I am one of the lucky ones, relatively speaking. The last time I was flying out of Montenegro's TGD airport, an older woman with two large sturdy reusable shopping bags as carry-ons was sitting next to me waiting for the boarding call. We started talking when she asked me where the toilets were and if I would keep an eye on her things for a minute. She was flying to Italy, it turned out, to visit her daughter who works as a personal support worker, taking care of a bed-ridden older woman. The bags were packed with homemade food, the Balkan delicacies that the daughter probably misses in Umbria or wherever, wrapped in multiple layers of aluminum foil and plastic bags —overwrapped, like the sandwiches my mother would insist I take on my long train trip back to Belgrade when I was a student. This was the woman's first time at the airport. She was nervous she would take a turn down a wrong corridor, or open a door she was not supposed to. In the event, I waved at her as she was lining up, slightly flustered, in the right queue at the gate for the Rome flight.

I met a death doula last year, after the talk she gave at a public library about the decisions that need to be made before one's death, and the options facing those who lose someone. It was near the end of an almost five-year period during which I couldn't stop being aware of death and its demands on life. I've walked around Toronto cemeteries, my awareness of not having a plan if death strikes right at this moment, today or tomorrow, weighing on me. The trouble with not having a friend in virtue, a serious friend, is that it means not having a local emergency contact; all the places of employment, volunteering, and even fitness establishments ask for someone to contact if you happen to sign off while on their premises. It means not having a person locally for the end-of-life and after life administration. Solo immigrants have more to reflect on and consciously decide, even after death. There's that additional decision to make: where to be buried? Here or the old country. And if the conscious choice of where to spend one's last days is not an option, if the death is unexpected, there should be a plan in place.

Graves with Chinese lettering in Mount Pleasant Cemetery bring me strange relief. Ah good, there are foreigners who were buried here, not of this soil but buried in it, it's been done, it's doable. There are those who have decided to stay and return to the elements here.

Before the autumn of 2015, I hadn't been called to ponder death very much, or to notice how uprooted I really am. Those were endlessly postponable, and anyway fixable, questions. When my mother died in October that year, it was as if the implacable one of the three Greek Fates, Atropos, cut more than a thread of life. It slashed into my rooting and belonging protocols. They turned out to be such stuff as dreams are made of. Suddenly, everything was much later than I realized, distances much longer. Death is the cruelest of uprooting. I will now try to write about it.

Chapter 8

THAT OCTOBER, when my mother died, I have a dentist appointment in the calendar the week after I return to Toronto. I decide to keep it. I ride my bicycle to the detached house in upper Bloor West Village next to the entrance to Baby Point. I park at the usual traffic-sign pole out front.

It's been a while, the dentist tells me. He pokes around my mouth, suggests preventive X rays because it has been too long since the last ones. He finds a chipped filling, proposes a re-fill. Not this time? Okay, I'll have the receptionist book you for another time. He begins the cleaning.

Tooth by tooth, one inner row of teeth then its outer side, the rounded hook slides between the gums and the roots, millimetre by millimetre. The pain is of the minor kind that's almost pleasurable. Plaque debris falls off, and when there is too much of it, the swish of water and the water sucker. Scratch, whoosh. Methodically, tooth by tooth. He takes his time.

I have dental insurance thanks to my two-day-a-week office job in a building in Etobicoke. When I first got it and could pay for regular trips to the dentist, I pooled recommendations and went to the little house in

Bloor West with a cheerful stock photo on the sign outside. The dentist is deeply involved, determined that no trace of plaque on his patient's teeth will remain. I open my eyes and in the strong lights notice spots of sweat on his forehead. 'I'll tell you about this instrument,' I remember he said when we met for the first time. 'This instrument is used to break cement in construction. I only take it out in cases of serious calcification.' He wasn't joking.

That was some years earlier. My teeth are cleaned regularly now. He continues to fuss. I lie passive, mouth wide open, a body fussed over, a set of teeth diligently, preventively cleaned. What used to come to mind during those occasions was the dentistry of the communist era I'd experienced as a child. Communist-era dentistry sounds like an insufferable indie band, but I am not saying it for the laughs. It was different. Much of it fine, but no anaesthetic. Painful drilling was quite an ordinary thing, something to get through, a regular experience at the dentist. Only unreasonably fussy or fragile people asked for a freeze before drilling.

This time, no, I do not think of that: I think of my mother's teeth. Let me see them, open up, I asked her on a walkabout in the apartment, three days before she died. She was weakening fast and nobody could tell us why. She was increasingly sleepy and unwilling to get up, so I made her walk to the bedroom, and we looked at the courtyard behind our concrete mid-rise. As someone newly converted to the science of preventive dentistry and the new owner of a mouth fussed over in a western high-income country, private-insurance kind of way, I told her that once she felt better she must see a dentist and have a proper clean and ask about those little grooves, what on earth causes them, and how do we take care of them?

She gave scant attention to my insistence. I talked, she pretended to listen. She wanted to walk back to the daybed in the living room. She would be returned to the hospital the next morning.

I lie with my mouth open while the dentist continues to put all his effort into the task. What precious teeth I have, in my well-taken-care-of body. Scratch scratch scratch scratch scratch scratch, then spit the saliva flecked with red, and the pain is near delightful.

* * *

Bodies keep the sediments of history, nothing dissolves. The hospital where my mother died is the one where I was born. Newer wings have opened, but the central building still stands. I was always sick with tonsillitis and always getting antibiotic shots for it. Am I six? I'm six, or five, or nine. Pills were often attempted, but did not work and we'd go right to the series of shots next time. Six shots, and mother would let me skip the sixth. It's a tradition we had. Out of all those shots, the one time that my father took me stands out. What could have happened? Was she sick? It was an unnatural state of affairs in that I couldn't show emotions with my father accompanying me. It was a lousy outing. In the old hospital wing, named after the founder of the dynasty Petrović. Shots were a regular part of childhood.

I remember mom's migraines well, and that I had headaches too. I'd be bed-ridden sometimes. I distinctly remember darkened windows and daybeds. Was I participating in her life this way? Solidarity, imitation? First procedure of feminine helplessness?

Later in life, she was the healthy one when dad's chronic illness started accelerating. She administered what needed to be administered. Planned medication, cleaned wounds. The keeper of the secret of just how sick he was, because he was adamant that he wasn't. For all of my adulthood, my dad was desperately hard of seeing and desperate for nobody to notice. Frailty was shameful and needed to stay hidden.

How far away his death feels. He's still a puzzle. There are moments now when I am certain that if I had lived with or married a woman while he was alive and had the courage to introduce the situation, he'd have come around to it after the adjustment period. I imagine him in certain moments getting used to and secretly perhaps enjoying the novelty of this bizarre new woman-to-woman relationship that his youngest has settled in. In his sixties, he got curious about computers, while mom remained terrified of them. She did master the basics of email and Skype so we could stay in touch, but that's where it ended.

She bore him three daughters. I came ten years after the second one and, the family lore says, my sex was a disappointment. 'I always felt alone at the hospital after the birth,' my mother told me. 'Always sad in the hospital.' I don't expect Montenegrin fathers visited then and am not sure that they are very hands-on postpartum now.

The hometown hospital remains intact in memory and in actuality. The last time I was there, the four last days while mother was dying, I took a break, left the hospital room and walked to the common area on the ward. It looked unchanged since it was first filled with furniture decades before, back when smoking was allowed. Windows were open on that day, but there was smoke, lingering. What kind of a rebellion is smoking in a hospital? A way to stick it to the man, an instrument of freedom? I grew up with these people and am one of them: what is my smoking? What do I insist is the means of freedom, while it's nothing of the sort?

* * *

There were two other women in my mother's room. One, an older woman from the village between the town and the sea would unravel her braids and comb her long grey hair each morning. After I asked her if she wanted our newspapers, she calmly told me that she couldn't read, never got round to learning. I liked her. The other woman was younger and was there for some tests. She would often get phone calls from her son, who I figured lived in another city and had his own family. He did come to collect her when the time came. By then, the grey-haired old lady from the seaside had left as well. We were alone with mother in her last two days.

I noticed the TVs in the rooms immediately. Wait, there are televisions in hospital rooms in our hometown? It turns out the television sets were a donation from a foundation, or the EU, but the local authorities hadn't done their part and the TVs remained unconnected. Shiny new screens in each room, dead.

* * *

It is only fair, as the daughter who's been absent the most, that the task of the night shift falls to me. I do not complain. It is presumed, it is understood. Later I insist somebody join me, sister number two, the one who emigrated to a European country, could travel more and therefore had seen more of our mother than I had, but still less than our oldest sister, who stayed in the hometown all her life and was with our mother most frequently. The oldest can sleep in her own home. She has earned it.

* * *

For some time in 1914 and 1915, Swiss painter Ferdinand Hodler sat by his dying lover and painted. She was Valentine Godé-Darel, present in Hodler's earlier paintings that burst with colour and movement, but now she is supine and the colours are few. A great deal of drawings, studies and paintings of the sick and dying Valentine survive, scattered all around

Switzerland, in the museums of Bern, Zurich, Basel, Solothurn, and in private collections. It would be impossible to gather them all in one room and arrange them chronologically to follow her waning as it occurred.

Hodler must have worked incessantly. In the early paintings of Valentine seated in bed against white pillows, she returns the gaze and looks straight at the viewer. In later images, she lies in bed, eyes permanently closed, but she is breathing and sometimes changing positions. There are sketches of Valentine sleeping with head turned left, others with head turned right, mouth closed or open. She gets thinner and thinner, after a certain point entirely immobile. Hodler kept coming back, shaping what was before his eyes into lines on paper. Since Valentine liked roses, they appear in some images as red spots near her bed, interrupting the whites and the greys.

The near-dead and the dead Valentine appear in slightly different styles. We are not spared anything. All the changes of the flesh are recorded. The elongated figure of a woman will for some bring to mind Holbein's dead Christ in the tomb and offer an out: the depiction is unbearably realistic. There's a door into art history which one can take to get away from the body, but it's only available to those who come prepared. Most of us arrive unequipped with such an education and have no escape.

The dead are not rare in paintings. There are many depicting Christ, the war dead, and the murdered. What is rare in painting is the march of time, the passage to the other side. Hodler witnessed it, and makes us witness Valentine's inexorable waning and her body's assumption of the mask of death. Valentine's face is different after the exit of Valentine the person and Hodler does not avoid showing this.

Art and language largely fumble before a dying and dead body, or avert the gaze. There are exceptions. Annie Leibowitz photographed Susan Sontag in her last days. Mijke de Jong's docudrama film *Frailer* follows one of her close friends through terminal illness to the other side and remains looking after she dies, without pulling the curtain. What is gathered, what is learned? I have no philosophical insight to offer, said the actress Holland Taylor of the death of her own mother. One moment the person was there, the next she wasn't. It's like looking at the ocean, the sky, a mountain massif: you are awed and humbled, but can anything really be said, can silence ever be improved on?

* * *

When I return to Toronto that October, my life strikes me as a business thoroughly unreal. A pretence; playing house. I slow down on the bicycle. Late at night, after a concert, riding northbound, putting my face in a silent Munch scream feels good. Uncared for, the streets are full of holes and bumps. The uncaring of late-night cyclists. Past the Greek church on Sorauren Avenue, I think of stopping by and lighting a candle, an empty gesture—she was atheist, as am I—out of a need for ritual. I do not. There are no secular grieving rituals to be found. Somebody recommends a grieving group run by a retired palliative nurse who immediately responds to my email. They sometimes release butterflies, I learn, in honour of those who passed. They sometimes meet and talk. I never go.

What I am probably looking for is a sand or mud pit to roll in. I am looking for a shaman to return me to my body. Somebody to yell at me to wake up. Switch the senses on. A few things still ask for my presence, so I show up—a writing assignment for a magazine, the secretarial job in the suburbs. When there is nothing, there is always the indomitable dullness of the clerical job, so I go to that. I struggle to stay awake at the opera. Between acts one and two, I stop paying attention to the stage and work hard to stay conscious. It's a tidal blackening.

It started in Vienna, where I flew to use up my vacation before returning to Toronto. One can never afford to not use vacation; there is not much allowance for it, and once missed it will not come back. Therefore one must use it or lose it. Use the vacation, serf, use it, *use it*. Vienna was Bruges-la-Morte for four days. The garishness and the gilt on stage, the TV iconicity of the Musikverein concert hall. I left the Staatsoper at intermission; the Verdi Macbeth sounded incongruously cheerful for a tragedy. WTF is a chipper dance beat doing in this score?

Back in Toronto, it continues. Concerts and operas emptied of content. There is nobody I can tell. Those I try to tell in the coming years will not really hear it. You don't really hear the news of the death of another person's mother unless you've experienced the equivalent yourself. I remember an acquaintance some years ago mentioning in a piece of professional email communication that she took some time off after her mother died, and I remember feeling presented with something almost obscene, a raw emotion I didn't ask for, the enormity of which was outside my grasp. How strange to have this piece of information presented to me, I thought. And now I am presenting it in the same way to unsuspecting others, until I stop. There is no point in that. I cannot be heard, so I stop telling.

I am not exactly left alone: death is close, the mouth breather, no respect for personal space. It is coming, I am damn sure of it. It's close and not only for me, but for others who have lost the capacity to see it. Plans need to be made for when I die with no family around for the last decisions or goodbyes. I manically look for cases in literature of women dying alone, women who love other women dying alone, or permanently unpaired women, and cannot find anything for a while. Then, one find: Margaret Edson's *W;t*. While it's never specified whether the play's protagonist is lesbian or other, the playwright, in fact, is. It has been written, then.

It exists, it is not unheard of. It is known. It is not unspeakable, or an agonizing scandal. I must find other women in literature who lived full lives and were not afraid of dying alone—and have died alone.

The cemetery in my hometown — the main one — never slips my mind as the never abandoned ghostly alternative, a parallel death and burial. Beautiful stone graves, austere and imposing, letters carved by the one craftsman that everybody employs. The pine tree next to my parents' place of rest. Four names, my mother's added last. Since I remain the unmarried daughter who is not joining her husband's family's resting place, it could be my spot too. Phantasmically. Possibly. Would I return to be buried there? But why, I wonder. Fewer and fewer people know me there and extremely few will know me there when I die. To be buried here in Canada, then, so far away? My dying is at an impasse at the moment, up in the air. Place marker. I mustn't die before this is decided. I'll have to do my all not to.

* * *

Between the ages of sixteen and twenty-one, my mother watched every movie released in the cinemas of northern Montenegro, and, after getting married and moving south, continued to watch films on television. It's how I got to know at a very young age the names of people like Clarke Gable, Jimmy Stewart, Robert Mitchum, Katherine Hepburn, Ginger Rogers, Fred Astaire, Gene Kelly, and Marilyn Monroe. Much happened in the history of cinema from those days to the eighties when I was growing up, and my mother continued to follow new filmmaking until the country's economy took a dive. Local *kino* closed for good, the newly created commercial TV channels ceased buying quality films, and digitization and the internet brought to the region an era of wholesale piracy which is still in effect to a degree. Her interests expanded (Omar Sharif, Robert de Niro, Al Pacino, Jeanne Moreau, Jean-Paul Belmondo, Jean-Louis Trintignant, Monica Vitti, Marcello Mastroianni, Sofia Loren) but the Old Hollywood movies from her youth remained hers. (The way I now consider the 1980s and 1990s in pop music mine, although I've since moved on.) Even after it's been implicitly agreed in the family, likely because my father thought it so, that cinephilia is a silly pursuit, a clutching at shadows, my mother kept at it, atypically ignoring our judgment. She and I watched a lot of things together.

Over the years, her favourite films became David Lean's visual epics. *Dr Zhivago*, but most of all *Ryan's Daughter*. I have asked her many times at various junctures what her favourite film was, and I remember *Ryan's Daughter* always among the select few. She hadn't travelled much since marrying, and then only to visit extended family in Zadar, Kraljevo, Tuzla, and Belgrade (all cities in the former Yugoslavia). The vast landscapes of Lean's cinematographer, Freddie Young, must have appealed. I watched the film again recently, and the emotions in it are at least as big as the vistas, Sturm und Drang-ness perhaps overboard. But not if you're anchored in the increasingly grey former royal capital of Montenegro for fifty years, where you know you will stay until you die. *Ryan's Daughter* is loosely based on *Madame Bovary*, with Sarah Miles's character much less humiliated by the narration than Flaubert's heroine, much more sympathetic and joyously drawn, her actions not really the result of bingeing on bad novels but of a dream for a more fulfilling relationship. She survives the publicizing of her love affair, her husband staying by her side through the village walk of shame. The illicit liaison is a ripple of the First World War, which for the most part happened far from Ireland. There is ostracism as a cathartic shoring up of a small community. There is a very operatic storm—Lean waited for an actual one to film the scene in which the villagers recover the boxes of ammunition from the ocean for the Irish Republican Brotherhood. Most of the film was shot on the beaches of the Dingle Peninsula. Rugged, vast, wrapped in lush green, weather cruel and moody, they differ from the beaches of Montenegro in all respects but sand and water. A book of oral history about the very eventful filming of the last big 'blank-cheque' studio film, Paul Benedict Rowan's *Making Ryan's Daughter: The Myths, Madness and Mastery,* came out in Ireland in 2020. (Naturally, I own it.) What could my mother have appreciated the most in this film, I often wonder, and I suspect it's the stubborn, free spirit in the girl, the escapism of it, since my mother's settled life was secure and confined.

Another film that we watched together now stands out as important: *Stage Door* with Katherine Hepburn, Ginger Rogers, and no male protagonist or romance. Directed by *My Man Godfrey*'s Gregory La Cava, it's a workplace dramedy, except set at home, at an all-female *pensionnat* for young actresses. How could I have never asked her what life was like in her own pensionnat? Mothers don't have a life before we are born. If it's ever brought up, we don't listen. It pales as a prehistory before family record keeping.

Had I watched *Doctor Zhivago* while she was alive, I would have been intrigued to find another complicated female character in one of her favourite films. (Doctor Zhivago, *because* mother liked it, plummeted down the cultural priority list, and took the Pasternak novel it was based on with it.) Once you take away Maurice Jarre's overbearing one-tune score, *Zhivago* is a fine film, made for the grown-ups. Did she feel an affinity for Lara, even if the character was a photographic negative of her own life choices? How independent, alive, and flawed in all directions Lara was, I thought when I finally saw the movie on my laptop (a crime against cinematography).

From the depth of memory creeps this thought: mother didn't allow us to wear makeup, including nail polish, to school. I remember—or re-inscribe retrospectively? Surely not. I remember that was the only period when I was genuinely interested in experimenting with makeup. It was the eighties, too, with MTV videos and The Cure and Boy George and Annie Lennox. It all became less interesting and less pressing once I got out and went to university. It was rare for mother to issue non-negotiable prohibitions, but I remember this one clearly. I expect the prohibition came because mother thought that nail polish and makeup meant sexualisation, dating men, and readying yourself for men, but I don't think that's why I was interested. Was it peer pressure, was I eager to be like other girls in the class, many of whom miraculously switched from the innocence of grade school to boyfriends in middle school? At any rate, mother absolutely had a petty bourgeois—or more plainly, a terrified—view of pre-university dating. Whatever she thought of Ryan's daughter and Lara, their view of morals and female freedom didn't spill over into her life as a wife and mother. I could have rebelled. My older sisters had rebelled in their time, but then their rebellions passed from view, like a comet, not a precedent. There were more than ten years between us, and with me everything started anew.

Another memory. I'm in my twenties, more independent now, a senior student in Belgrade, back in Montenegro for the summer vacation. I find myself with mother and one of her old friends and her family in a town on the coast. It's somewhere in the Bay of Boka, a pleasant beach, enclosed by the mountains. A small island with a church sits between the two sides of the bay. I remember swimming out, to a point, and wondering if I should swim all the way to the island. There is nothing to it really, maybe one kilometre in all, and there would be no hurry to return; we'll be here on the beach all day. But when I had broached the idea with my mother earlier, she had answered for me: of course you will not, it is dangerous (it wasn't). I stopped, trod water, thought about her words, hated myself for complying, hated her for instilling her own fears in me, turned around and swam back.

Three years later, I went away to a place incomparably more distant. She wasn't happy, but generally abetted my escape, perhaps thinking that it would not be permanent. Five years in, ten years in, even after I took Canadian citizenship, she kept asking over the phone: yes, but when are you coming back? She died, my chatterbox aunt told me last time I saw her, still longing for the two of her daughters who emigrated. It used to make me mad, hearing things like that. Is our purpose on earth to please our mothers? Assuage their yearnings for wholeness? Never separate, or separate only nominally? Mother, I thought, has been astounded by the gall of my—our —going away, the abandonment. I was sure the ties had to be cut. There was no freedom otherwise. No mother and father, no blood and soil of the Balkans, I must be alone, create my own life from the beginning. One should find a way to translate the body's nocturnal memories, preserved in the mother tongue, into the new language. But why bother translating, I thought, if you can still function brilliantly, thrive obviously? *Quand on n'est nulle part, on pense. Quand on n'est nulle part, on écrit.* When we are nowhere, that's where the thinking and writing begin.

* * *

There's one big difference between Margaret Edson's play *W;t* and the film based on it, *Wit*, with Emma Thompson. The character Vivian Bearing, a professor of English and a specialist in the Holy Sonnets of John Donne, receives a stage 4 cancer diagnosis. Being treated in a research hospital and herself a scholar, she agrees to a severe experimental treatment for the sake of medical research and human knowledge, and to increase her chances of survival. We observe her losing individuality in the hospital and becoming an instance of biometrically observable matter. This inexorable process is interrupted only by flashbacks— memories of her studying and teaching—and the verses of John Donne. Parts of Sonnet 10 recur:

> Death be not proud, though some have called thee
> Mighty and dreadful, for, thou art not soe,
> For, those, whom thou think'st, thou dost overthrow,
> Die not, poore death, nor yet canst thou kill me.
> From rest and sleep, which but thy pictures be,
> Much pleasure; then from thee much more must flow
> And soonest our best men with thee do go,
> Rest of their bones, and soul's delivery.
> Thou 'art slave to Fate, chance, kings, and desperate men,
> And dost with poyson, warre, and sicknesse dwell,
> And poppie or charmes can make us sleepe as well
> And better than thy stroake; why swell'st thou then?
> One short sleep past, wee wake eternally,
> And death shall be no more, Death, thou shalt die.

In an early memory, Vivian's favourite teacher gives her a drilling over a paper, starting with the edition she used. The punctuation is all wrong, and putting exclamation points in the last verse is unnecessary hysterics, Professor Ashford is adamant. Death shall be no more—comma: "Nothing but a breath—a comma—separates life from life everlasting. It is very simple, really. With the original punctuation restored, death is no longer something to put on a stage, with exclamation points. It's a comma, a pause . . . Life, death. Soul, God. Past, present. Not insuperable barriers, not semicolons, just a comma."

To which student Bearing does not reply, "Well, yes if you're a Christian; otherwise no." In the film and in the play, she promises to do a better job and goes back to the library. "It is *not wit*, Miss Bearing. It is truth. The paper's not the point."

The *it is truth* part of this does not appear in the screenplay by Mike Nichols and Emma Thompson. Nor does Vivian, in the last scene of the film, get up and walk toward the light, as she does in the play. She dies the same way she does in the play, but there is no light to rise to. Compared to the play, the film is agnostic about how much truth there is in Donne's sonnets. The religious nature of the verses wasn't given a rubbishing except through what we see, a body in the agony of dying. Salvation and redemption are poetic conceits which one may or may not choose. Are religious people happier and less afraid of dying? Donne, in the play, is a drug which works until it doesn't, when Dr Bearing becomes too sick for poetry and intellectual analysis. Retired Prof. Ashford, who turns out to be a well-adjusted human with a family and grandchildren, is in town on other business and visits her in the hospital. I suspect we naturally like Dr. Ashford because she's played in the film by Eileen Atkins; her religious certainty and successes in heterosexuality would irk more if this was another actor. Shall I recite something for you, she offers, to which the half-conscious Vivian groans *nooo*. So Ashford lies next to her and reads from a picture book.

That picture book about the runaway bunny who decides not to run away after all, as his mother would always be there beside him whatever shape he takes so he might as well stay put, turns out to be a Christian allegory, too. Is this absurd or comforting to Vivian? Ashford is a mother, Vivian isn't; one won't die alone, the other one will. Apart from the one visit from Ashford, Edson gives Vivian no other visitors while she's in the hospital. After a particularly hard bout of retching early in the treatment,

Vivian relaxes to some sarcasm. "God, I'm going to barf my brains out . . . If I actually did barf my brains out, it would be a great loss to my discipline. Of course, not a few of my colleagues would be relieved. To say nothing of my students."

Margaret Edson is a public school teacher in her late fifties. She is partnered to a woman and they have two children. She has no intention of writing another thing. When asked about it, she says that she had said what needed saying, and her life is fulfilling as is.

* * *

The first time I return to the now permanently empty apartment to see if I can sort the objects that concern me (my sisters would have done most of their own sorting by that time), I come across an old book with my mother's maiden name on the first page. The handwriting, in ornamented, almost calligraphic Cyrillic lettering, is that of a young woman. The book impressum shows the year 1959, so she is at least nineteen, already a boarder at the kindergarten teachers' college in the still fairly new communist Yugoslavia. She will be married in two years, and have my oldest sister in 1962. It's the period of her life I know least about. It's also the one with most promise. Few objects from that time survive. Except, it appears, this textbook.

Called *Washing and Ironing*, it's part of a series published by the Central Institute for the Improvement of the Household in the People's Republic of Slovenia. It has been translated from Slovenian into Serbo-Croatian for the students in teacher training and household management, but equally for housewives across the new forward-looking nation. (In the previous Yugoslavia, which was a monarchy, about 60 percent of women were illiterate; the post-war communist regime set out to fix this.) The first half of *Washing and Ironing* is dedicated to the handling of textiles, underwear and outerwear, types of water, soap, and detergent available, manual washing techniques and air drying, bleaching and colouring, and the maintenance of long-lasting clothes. It is only by the second half, about washing clothes in machines, that I begin to see the purpose of the book. Most women at the time washed the laundry by hand, and those who could afford it hired a washerwoman to wash the family laundry manually. The textbook was meant to educate a reluctant generation of women, and their children's teachers, on the advantages of machine washing. *Washing is moving from the household into the communal washing facilities*, was the title that opened the second half. "As the number of women who work outside the home is increasing, the time available for the domestic tasks is decreasing. Therefore, we should endeavour to move as much of the domestic work outside the home. With social progress, a good number of such jobs (for example, weaving, dough making, canning, bread baking etc.) has already moved to the trades and industry, and what remains in the household is the upkeep of the apartment and the furniture, washing, cleaning of the textiles, and making food."

The opening chapter of the second half goes on to address anti-machine prejudices, and to argue in favour of creating machine washing centres, either individual ("but this is an unaffordable investment for most households"), or within buildings, or larger centres for entire blocks. There are chapters that break down how the washing machines work, how they are installed and serviced, and a final section dedicated to the already existing state-run manufacturers of washing machines and cleaning products. The familiar, widely used brands from the communist era survived until the end of the planned economy, with extremely few surviving the transition into the new world of privately-owned companies.

During my time as a student in the rapidly changing Belgrade under Milošević in the early 1990s, I learned of an old downtown building of apartments without kitchens. The idea was that cooking, too, would move out into the public sphere—or, at least, a communal space where it could become a joint responsibility for more people than one's family unit. Things did not go that way and in due course the building became an eccentricity. Apartments with private kitchens continued to be the norm and the new economy achieved a level of prosperity that allowed for individual washing machine ownership and a Yugoslav version of consumerism.

What did my mother and her friends make of this handbook? Was it already outdated then? Was it a subject to mock and pretend to take seriously until you got a good grade, or was the intent behind it understood as genuine, and respected? I couldn't tell.

Communism, however, was real for her father, and her father's brother, before it was the actual political system of the entire country. Both men died during the war of liberation of Axis-occupied Yugoslavia and Montenegro. She barely ever had memories of her dad, who was killed when she was a toddler. Her uncle's short life is somewhat better documented and his page in the People's Liberation War Heroes chronicles of Tito's communist Yugoslavia is now also on Wikipedia, in Cyrillic lettering. "Comes from an impoverished peasant family." Indeed: that was my mother's family's class background, although the situation got significantly brighter in her youth when she lived in a small house with her widowed mother and two sisters. The uncle found purpose, education, and extended family in the Communist Party of Yugoslavia's mobilization of the downtrodden in the pre-war monarchy, and during the Second World War occupation.

My mother never really knew her father, my sisters and I never had a maternal grandfather, and the first-generation communists never got a chance to see what came out of the liberation struggle. Never got to see the volunteering youth brigades who rebuilt after the devastation, the fast industrialization of a predominantly rural country, and the somewhat forced modernization and anti-tribalism. They also never got to see the formation of what Milovan Djilas described as the New Class, nor the detention camp on the island of Goli Otok after Tito broke away from Stalin, nor the prosperity or how it all came crashing down in the reignited flames of tribalism and the original accumulation of capital.

Mother would probably have had a father and an uncle had they not joined the resistance. But since it's the depth of the Balkans in the first half of the twentieth century, one must ungenerously ask: would their presence have limited her freedom, or enhanced it? Would they have been loving or tyrannical?

At the age of sixteen, my mother left her parental home and moved to the *pensionnat* at a teachers' college, where the optimistic textbooks on the mechanized and socialized future of housework awaited her. She would be married by the age of twenty-one. There was at least some life to live for her, and her only.

* * *

When I leave Junction and move to an east end apartment, the bereavement dials up to acute. At one point, I map out the mental health service centres. For no reason, I say to myself; perhaps to see if I can volunteer eventually. The distress centre for short stays is a spacious old house painted baby blue. It has survived the over-development of Charles St. East and is itself seemingly not distressed. Further south on Jarvis, I notice a neutral looking building pointed at by the sign Community Mental Health Centre. And between Shuter and Queen streets, I take note of St Michael's Hospital's emergency entrance, just as an fyi to self.

So that is now my closest large hospital. Say you need to stay the night under supervision, can you check yourself in? Just walk in, say I need to be looked after for a while or I will do something incredibly stupid, like punch a man who insulted me in a supermarket queue this morning—it almost happened (it did happen in my head)—or I can decide to sleep and never leave the bed. There is an angel on a banner on St Michael's south wall, but there are no urban stories with angels left for Toronto. L.A. and Berlin took the angels. This was a place bombed out by construction sites, endless skeletons of towers empty of meaning, waiting to be filled.

* * *

The bus negotiated the serpentines well until it couldn't. The bus drove merrily until it lost control over itself, broke through the road safety fence and tumbled into the canyon. It tumbled and while tumbling all the way down it rolled. It rolled and flipped like tumbleweed. Like a ping pong ball missing the edge of the table, down it went before any passengers inside could begin to notice. Those inside might have been sleeping; it was a familiar drive for most, including the driver, who nevertheless lost control. Was it the steering, was it the narrow road, did a tire fall off, was there a stone avalanche? Down went the bus, and fast, and when the people inside noticed and started to scream, it was near the end, when the bus flipped again and hit an obstacle on the mountainside. Was it shrubbery that it got stuck in? It stopped, but not before having tumbled all its insides, heads hitting seats and floor and ceiling, overhead luggage spilling out, people falling on each other, melee, melee. Was the radio on, did it continue playing as they all tumbled, and was it turbo folk, or something more pleasant. Or was it, unprecedentedly, a silent vehicle?

Mother was inside that bus, sitting probably in one of the aisle seats, in the front section, I expect, on her way from my hometown to the capital, or vice versa. Nothing could be more routine. The murmur of the conversations from the other passengers, the sunset among the mountains, overcast or clear; or maybe it was earlier on a plain day, no special weather conditions. Dry roads. Traffic on the roads not excessive. Traffic on the road reasonable, in fact. One moment the driver is in perfect control of the enormous steering wheel, next moment the tons of steel, gas, and rubber has a mind and momentum of its own which the driver could not foresee, even though, let's grant him the benefit of the doubt, he was not micro-sleeping, he was sober, he drank nothing at all that day, and his cell phone was off and tucked away.

The bus skidded. The bus flew off the road. Did mother hold on to her armrests? When a confined group of people all believe they are dying, each running a tape of the life passed, do their tapes merge in some way, the busload of life tapes running fast from birth to that very moment of flying off a cliff?

As the bus begins to descend, mother runs her images, which I cannot guess. I expect her daughters are there. She could be running each of us on parallel simultaneous reels—well, only partly simultaneous, my older sisters running on their own for the ten years and twelve years ahead of me. But it ought to have been her own life, running fast as the bus is descending. Her own life back into the present where she is facing death, or so she thinks; she the author of it, us three only side reels. There should be her own reel of celluloid film, that she authored, independent of us, a magnificent one, full of colour and peaks and valleys and unpredictable heroines of their own stories.

Two hours later, she opened her eyes to the hospital wall. They survived, against all odds, every passenger, and some months later they will receive modest compensation for their misfortune. But now her mind is blank and her body is under hospital sheets. My oldest sister and her family are there, presumably.

I presume because I wasn't there. I was away, in Canada. I'm informed through email one day later. I'm told everything is all right, except for minor scratches and the shock.

I can't remember a single thing about this episode. All these details are imagined. Have I ever talked to her about it? I can't tell. I retain nothing, if ever I did ask about it. How could this not have been important enough for memory retention? I don't understand my own brain.

When I was five, and alone at home with my middle sister, I decided on my own to take something from the fridge, which was high up on a platform inside the pantry. When my little hands pulled the door, they pulled the entire old fridge over on top of me, trapping me inside and pushing the larder door shut. A vase, I remember, hit me on the forehead and broke skin. Other things must have broken around me, but I'm not sure what. I remember observing in astonishment this new situation.

At any rate, the door was unscrewed from the frame and I was liberated from the embrace of the fridge, relatively unscathed.

I survived the fridge tip-over, she survived the bus summersault. As I have no preserved information about my mother's brush with death, I am unearthing an episode that chimes with the one from decades earlier. My fridge, her bus, flying in opposite directions and I'd like to think crossing paths, as if in a Chagall painting.

* * *

In the first century of the new era, where now lies the state of Montenegro, lay the Illyrian state Doclea. Not long into its recorded history, it became one of the eastern provinces of the Roman Empire, Praevalitana, whose territory almost matches the current Montenegro. Its capital Doclea was near the meeting of two rivers in a vast pleasant plane encircled by gentle hills. I expect the climate was as moderately Mediterranean as it is today, and the soil equally fertile. The archaeological digging started near the end of the nineteenth century, and continued on and off when the governments were in the mood. The clearly gridded foundations of an entire Roman town square and its surrounding buildings remain to this day and are easy to wander about. Everything is open and unsupervised, although mapped by archaeologists and introduced to visitors via modest explanatory panels that are beginning to discolour and dampen under lamination. Some nations make a fuss of their ancient heritage, others don't. There are pieces of buildings scattered about, fallen ornaments, parts of monuments, short columns. The passages and what remains of windows and doors have clearly been designed to show the natural surroundings as beautiful and worth contemplating. Through the narrow window in a crumbling wall, I see the racing clouds between two hills and the view is lively and of the present day. They have predicted us and how we will see this territory. They knew what would last.

After the novelty of the first digs wore off, no subsequent government took a devoted interest in Doclea—not the monarchs, not the communist rulers, not the nationalists, and definitely not the current free marketers. The ghost-town square, to this day, stays wide open to the changes of weather and any intruders, human or animal. The land remains underexplored. The coins and the hair combs, the rings and the drinking cups, remain buried. Bus tours stay away, guides remain unemployed, books of Doclean history, social and political, remain unwritten. The plots of land owned by present-day Montenegrins in the current capital sprawl closer and closer to the edges of the ancient town square. A train track was laid through, the nearby inter-city roads widened. Every so often, traces of Doclea emerge on someone's private property. The owner of a vineyard or a large garden interrupts his building plans after his shovel clinks against what turns out to be a tombstone. Behind a garage, a workshop, a shed (if one knows where to look), there are graves of the people who once lived in now phantom edifices on the phantom square of Doclea. I saw half a dozen ancient graves, one with a stone coffin perfectly recovered by a professional hand and left there, as if the interest suddenly waned, on a piece of land which was meant to be somebody's vineyard but had to be given over to the centuries past. Next to it there's a functioning vineyard on extremely uneven ground—protrusions in the land that could easily be burial mounds, if anybody bothered to look. Above them, the vines soak up the warmth and grow the grapes undisturbed, and those grapes ferment to wine. Under a lively peripheral borough of Montenegro's capital, ancient bones sleep undisturbed. Invisible, undescribed, forgotten. And yet present, so many of them, with their artifacts, and buildings that survive the onslaught of centuries like nothing that we ourselves built ever will. At the meeting point of the two rivers, just as the hills become a plain.

* * *

One time, in Munich, I came across an exhibition of Alfred Kubin's works. Has anybody caught darkness better? The psychosis that are dreams, the porousness of the borders between human and animal, human and monstrous, and the presence of death, impossible to hide from view? There are figures who slaughter in some drawings, chopping bodies into parts. The blind march of war, in one, with hoofs against the ground. A lady riding a rocking horse with blades that cut humans. The release of an epidemic like dust over a town, singlehandedly, by a long-haired, elderly corpse. Then there is individual death. By the torturers' hands, a starved body leaving the tail of its own colon behind, or being dragged, by its captors. With a sharp object protruding from the back of his neck, a figure crawls up enormous stairs towards a crescent moon, by the gate formed by two naked creatures with tiny heads on top of round trunks with female genitals but male legs.

There is a shade-blanketed town square in *The Dying City*, with a row of buildings falling forward. A bed and a chair in the middle of the square, but nobody around. The year the work was made is 1905, the Great War not yet near, the carpet-bombing of the Second World War even farther off, but Kubin sees.

Head cut off and placed against the body by its owner, so self-reflection can be possible. To look upon oneself, lucidly.

The *Hour of Death* depicts an actual clock, with heads for hours and swords for hands. Three have already been cut down, but this is Kubin, so they don't just roll off but fall into a skip put under the clock for that reason. Hygiene and organization in the face of the inevitable.

The Kiss shows a naked man in an ardent (or desperate) embrace, his head between a woman's thighs. She is, however, dead. She has gone some way into death as she is closer to a skeleton than a body that's recently died.

In Kubin, women's naked bodies, in particular, over-abound and are never self-contained. They are a tie-in with the out-of-body, otherworldly animal, and the multiple within one. In *Fertility*, a naked woman lies at a crossing of two roads, her enormous pregnancy taking up her body from knees to almost the neck. It's hard to tell if the babies in placentas, and those more blob-like things—perhaps embryos?—are showering upward from her, or downward into her. Are the babies filling the woman to suffocation? Or coming out of her while never depleting, never letting the body be self-contained?

In the drawing *The Spider*, the female spider with mons veneris visible and enormous tentacle-like arms commands a spider's web where a number of copulating couples have been caught. They are busy and do not really notice or begrudge their fate; perhaps it's not a web unto death, but a web of surveillance, and besides, there are bird-like creatures hovering above the scene that distract. Perhaps a drawing that's more pornographic than grotesque or abject or fear-drenched. Did Louise Bourgeois ever see it before embarking on her mother spiders, I wonder.

In *The Ape*, a naked woman is being held like a baby in diapers by an upright ape, with the primate's hand between the legs for lower support. The woman's head is partly in the ape's wide-open mouth. She either isn't alive or has no will to resist.

The Egg is harder to look at. A woman skeleton carries an enormous swollen belly—or is it her own egg resurrecting her? She stands next to an empty grave. She emits light, somehow, or is surrounded by it. There's a shadow behind her on the wall, kingly, indeterminate, but not hers. Somebody observing, or herself leaving a shadow that is its own creature, not her.

Kubin dedicates an endearing amount of care to the female mons. In *Serpent Nightmare* it is the discreet centre of the image and of the creature itself, a human female with the arms of a tiger and a serpent's head and tongue. The image, although named a nightmare, does not emit horror but a certain calmness. The body will stand. The paws will grasp and the tongue will flick. But the body will stand.

The Death Leap is perhaps Kubin's answer to Courbet's *The Origin of the World*. The woman's chin, breasts, and thighs appear neatly symmetrical around the cave of her opening. Toward it falls a minuscule male figure— Lilliputian against the Brobdingnag of the woman's body.

There were drawings I saw in Munich that I couldn't find in monographs later; smaller, more realist scenes and vistas, urban and pastoral, that Kubin covered with a dense net of lines as if with its own crib of darkness. And while the scenes are for the most part devoid of the monstrous, their atmosphere is on first sight much darker. This looks like my hometown under heavy rain, I thought when I looked at a few of them in Munich. Much later, back in Toronto, while leafing through a Kubin book at the reference library, one of those scenes re-emerged. *Recollection of My First Bosnian Journey, 1907,* said the caption. Yes, of course, he understood the Balkans are exactly like that and require exactly that kind of seeing. I don't dare look too closely at the matter protruding from the ground, nor into the sole person's skeletal face.

Let's see if there are further depictions of the South Slav Balkans. There is one from Montenegro! Except that *From Cattaro* (From Kotor, the Bay of Boka, Kingdom of Montenegro), also 1907, looks like an idyllic watercolour of a town called Perast near Kotor. Looming mountains, enclosing even, but not menacing. Bright, serene colours. How was it possible that Kubin had no anguish to paint in Southern Montenegro? I am puzzled.

* * *

When the fear of dying or being dead appears, it may be useful to consider the long centuries of human history before we were born. That earlier nothingness does not pain you, so why would the nothingness of the centuries ahead? We should try to contemplate the pre-human natural history, or even the history of the universe, or universes, before life on earth emerged. Does that thought come with a pang? It does not. Still, it's understandable that we grieve the future that we will not witness; our consciousness emerging in the meantime, and extinguishing.

Theoretical physics, existentialist philosophy, and metered music know time, probably more than any other kind of discipline. Mothers, too, who are recording every tock following every tick for a lifetime, from conception on. When mothers take leave of us, there are still the other three to turn to, physics, music, and philosophy.

Having abandoned the religious and metaphysical understanding of consciousness—and unwilling to reduce it to brain science—the twentieth century existentialists and phenomenologists left us some intriguing paradigms about the human in the world. When Sarah Bakewell first read Heidegger in her twenties, her "whole way of seeing the world was influenced by his raw amazement that there *is* something rather than nothing . . . by his notion of humans are a 'clearing' in which Being emerges into the light". Maurice Merleau-Ponty had different imagery: "consciousness . . . is like a 'fold' in the world, as though someone had crumpled a piece of cloth to make a little nest or hollow. It stays for a while, before eventually being unfolded and smoothed away."

Or are we a wave which passes some distance before crashing against the coast and returning to the sea? It's the death that makes us singular, because we will come to it alone: it will be ours and only ours and from it backward our life will be seen as completed. Human uniqueness is already being chipped away by AI, pandemics, animal rights activism. Alexa and Siri are already being used for companionship. Bots perform fundraising calls for our charities, offer to write email and text messages for us, select our CVs and even interview us. AI is used in news reporting by such organizations as the BBC and Bloomberg. Algorithms are used in court sentencing and policing, and sometimes show less bias than humans. Surgeons are using robotics because robot tools can reach what human hands can't.

There may come a time (liberalism's unplanned outcome?) when we won't be sure what's so special about us humans. Consciousness of our own mortality, we could offer. The dread and joy of the possibility of freedom.

The fact that we have come from the elements and to them we will return. Once past the gate, I, that is, my body, will return to the anonymity of non-singular nature. It's not my soul that embarks on a journey, writes Cees Nooteboom in his 1991 novel *The Following Story*, it's my body setting out to wander endlessly, "never to be ousted from the universe, and so it would take part in the most fantastic metamorphoses, about which it would tell me nothing because it would long since have forgotten all about me." Matter once housed me, but after me it will have other purposes.

Physicist Julian Barbour makes a valiant attempt to break up time and stall it in the nows. The flowing of time is an illusion, according to him; there are only moments, heaps of moments that are forming the universe. What gives us the illusion of time passing is that some moments contain memory of other moments; some moments are more plentiful than others. We see that we are getting older by comparing the image of us from a current moment with an image from another moment—we are dependent on our sight to intuit that time is passing. What we set our clocks to is other clocks, not to the passing of time itself, he insists. What we see as our fate is already finished and complete together with the universe. Because we can't grasp this completeness, we experience it as a progression toward something, our bodies and minds ticking in the beat of their own time, mistaking it for the universe's.

If all of the lives and deaths have already occurred or, rather, are contained in the inert universe, how does Barbour account for bereavement, one wonders? Or explain the moment that is the hour of death: a consciousness runs out of moments to experience, but continues as images in other people's moments. And what do we mourn when we mourn a person, or a home, when the heap of moments that is us takes a turn for the sombre?

I have greater affinity for the physicist Lee Smolin, for whom time is not an illusion; not on a universal scale, nor on an intimate one. Universes emerge in the progression of time, each with its own laws of operation, ours emerging when the conditions for its emergence came together. It is time and we are time. The forward motion, the growth, the fraying in the passage, the loss, is the primary and most accurate intuition we possess. Nothing is timeless.

* * *

In her book *Mothers*, Jacqueline Rose ponders the countless ways that all of us—societies, individuals—expect too much of mothers. Flawlessness, exclusive attention, power to fix problems. I'm thinking that's what I've been doing too: I've been expecting her to go on after death. I've been demanding that she do so, taking her death as a personal affront, abandonment: *Ah but the benevolent gaze over my life is gone.*

It was never meant to last forever. And at any rate it should have looked elsewhere for longer while it existed in life so that the separation would be easier for the child now that it's gone for good.

To be crushed by your mother's death is an unreasonable demand to receive mothering till the end of your life, beyond hers.

Chapter 9

AFTER THIRTY YEARS, Montenegro finally changed government in the general election of 2020.

Communism technically ended there in 1989, as in the rest of Europe, however Yugoslavia's constitutive states had previously toppled their rulers in pseudo-workers' demonstrations demanding a turn to ethno-nationalism. I've since been sceptical of mass demonstrations as a tool for furthering democracy, the exact opposite attitude to Canada's progressives. I've had to drum up enthusiasm for the WTO demonstrations in Quebec City and the anti-G20 protest in Toronto. And, after the early years of excitement, I've abandoned Pride. Partly it's the annual parade's tedium of a long procession of police districts, insurance companies, and banks. More significantly, it's the Pride's recent upset over the existence of public libraries, and comedy. Meanwhile, Montenegro introduced its first Pride in the mid-2010s: a walk of a few hundred people surrounded by thick cordons of police protection against very credible threats of violence. There, the bolshy spirit of Pride reappeared.

While the iron curtain appeared to be coming down in Yugoslavia during the late 1980s with the internal takeover by the nationalist cadre of communist parties in Serbia and Montenegro, the actual democratization stalled. The ruling party changed its name, acquired new leaders, and won the first set of elections in extremely favourable conditions. The group of people that took over Montenegro in the early 1990s frayed over time, lost one of its strongmen because he remained loyal to Serbia's Milošević, then another when state prosecutors could no longer ignore an illegally acquired real estate empire. But the core of the group remained, and ran the nation of 600,000. The core's family and friends and other well-connected prospered while the rest lived paycheque to paycheque, if they were lucky enough to be working. To this day in many regions of Montenegro, generations of families have been stuck in cycles of poverty. The coastal towns and the nation's capital saw wild, unregulated development, while the rest of the country languished. Dozens of factories and companies established in the communist era, a range of light and heavy industries, did not *transition* to the 'free market' era and shuttered instead. (What happened and who ended up with those assets and that capital was lost in the murky waters of transition economies.) With communism, manufacturing, too, was gone. Retail and tourism came in its place. And, with time, lucrative contracts in public works. Some of the old communist brands from Slovenia, Croatia, or Serbia survive to this day (Gorenje, Fructal, Podravka, Takovo). The Czech Škoda, now owned by the Volkswagen group, produced my father's car -- in which I learned how to drive in the summer of 1999. Not a single Montenegrin brand survived.

Between the nineties and 2020, the Montenegrin ruling party created a major legal scandal about once a year: an audio recording surfacing of an attempt to buy votes with cash in my own home town; a video recording of an under-the-table handover of tens of thousands of euros in party financing; a major public tender going to the prime minister's brother, who then sued the state for not honouring the contract and won millions of euros in compensation. But they kept winning elections, exerting immense influence on the public broadcaster and the largest daily paper. What also kept them in power for so long is the argument that they are the only ones capable of saving Montenegrin institutions form Serbian hegemonic expansion. The ruling establishment came to national pride late, but then appropriated it as though it were its own privatized stretch of sea shore. Succession talks with the EU inched nowhere fast, but the country did join NATO, completing the NATO surround of the Adriatic with Italy, Croatia, Montenegro, and Albania, a move that displeased Russia's allies in Serbia—and in Montenegro. The anti-regime protests would regularly flare up about every two years, set off by very different groups fighting for causes ranging from ecology to anti-corruption to Russophilia to pro Serbian-clericalism. Until, finally, a critical mass of discontent accumulated in the year of the pandemic, just in time for the 2020 election.

Because we liberals in the Balkans are never allowed any unequivocal joys, the new parliamentary majority consists of three coalitions which ideologically overlap on few issues and may disintegrate between the writing of this book and its publication. There is a big Christian-Democrat component in this mélange (or rather a melee) of parties, consisting of centrist, triangulating Christian Democrats, hard-right Serbian nationalists (harbouring the odd vocal QAnon believer in their midst), laissez-faire neoliberals, the greens, and a small, genuinely liberal-democratic anti-nationalist party which holds the balance of power and is managing to finagle its own political goals amid the cacophony. (We'll meet one of their four MPs in the next chapter.) What so far unites them is the wish to see the end of clientelism, the desire for a more independent judiciary, and a more transparent and responsible government on all levels. Whether another value will suddenly seem pressing enough for any of the coalition members to withdraw their support, remains to be seen. The party of the former thirty-year regime, now the largest opposition party, waits on the sidelines, expecting it to happen any day.

The recurring jokes and memes right after the election raised the question of who would purchase the official Maybach Mercedes automobiles that the previous government drove around in. There are few people in Montenegro who can pay for that kind of ostentation. When it became obvious that the regime, rated by the Freedom House as a hybrid rather than democratic, would not interfere with the peaceful transfer of power in parliament, a period of exuberance followed, with liberal-democratic meme-makers producing outstanding work. North American media have taken a dim view of the internet in the South Slav Balkans, at least since the election of Trump in 2016 and subsequent coverage of North Macedonian fake-news farms. That view was not improved by evidence in more recent years that Serbia's Aleksandar Vučić government used troll bots in election campaigns. But there is a liberal corner of internet activism in the region that is very vital, if in a minority.

The week I'm writing this, in December 2020, the first Montenegrin peaceful change of government by the ballot box since 1904 has finally taken place. Criticized by virtually every single MP in the governing coalition for wildly varying reasons, the cabinet was eventually voted in. The hard graft of compromise, and fair reporting about it, was just beginning. Meanwhile the old president stays on. Presidential elections are some way off, and Montenegro's strongman is staying for the duration of his mandate, observing, waiting for that one fatal move that will be the end of the new coalition.

* * *

Why did I leave?

Selfish self-preservation. Poverty. Hopelessness. Authoritarianism. Freedom from family.

The Montenegrin variant of patriarchy also propelled me; Milošević, Milošević's Montenegrins, the warring, the crime, the economic devastation.

Does economic development undermine the patriarchy or prop it up? Montenegro's post-communist transition to capitalist markets, the first accumulation of capital, returned workers rights to the nineteenth century. My oldest sister, like most of my extended family today, is working class. She has held a series of full-time service industry jobs in delis and hotels which entailed no weekends or sick days. My immediate family used to be lower-middle-class under communism, but it didn't entirely carry over to the next generation.

While some sociologists and philosophers question the usefulness of the all-encompassing concept of patriarchy, Montenegro is a case, I expect one of many in the world, where neither communism nor subsequent market liberalization managed to shake up a society structured along bloodlines, actual (family) or symbolic (*kumovi* and friends). Some researchers have argued that the close, unofficial *Gemeinschaft* relationships and connections function as a buffer against events and are resistant to change precisely because of so many political and legal changes taking place.

Until a better concept is found, I will continue to describe Montenegro as patriarchal. Communism did change some things. Free education from kindergarten to post-graduate level helped many women get outside the household and on a career path, as did government funded healthcare, and there were no massive gender wage gaps in the workforce of communist Yugoslavia. The gendered divide between STEM and the humanities seen in so many wealthy countries of the west did not take hold; engineering was an ordinary and fine career choice for women. The gender gaps among disciplines deepened, paradoxically, with gradual liberalization and the era of easy access to western advertising and media. But underneath the system of formal equality in employment, the patriarchal core remained. The Communist Party politburos did not produce female leaders who would be the equivalent of Tito, Ranković, Djilas, Kardelj, and similar figures. And in 2020, Montenegro remains one of the not insignificant number of countries around the world with a deficit in female births (48 percent to 52 percent), pointing to sex-selective abortions as the cause. One of the reasons I lost enthusiasm for the mainstream Canadian and American feminist activism, which favours gender self-identification and accepts as a woman any male who declares himself a woman, is that it disappears the language of sex-based activism which is essential in Montenegro and many other countries. It removes the vocabulary with which I can object to the female birth deficit.

Women under communism did just about all the child care, elder care (of the husband's family, too), and household chores. Work hours were from six or seven a.m. to two or three p.m., after which the family had lunch (planned, shopped for, and made by the mother, and as the children grew, daughters). My own father would retreat after lunch to his bedroom for a nap, Montenegro still being part of the siesta civilization circle of the Mediterranean, while my mother would proceed with dishwashing. It was a rotten deal. I realized this at about age eleven and—not understanding the system that was producing it, which Beauvoir wrote about in The Second Sex—proceeded to reject the women who went along with it, starting with my own mother.

My first move of detachment from my parents into individuation was an act of psychic aggression toward my mother, disdain for her life and her overbearingness while eating the food that she made and wearing the clothes that she washed. My two much older sisters rebelled against some things, but never against this fundamental setup. So I didn't either. I boycotted instead, which meant boycotting my mother. As Julia Kristeva points out, you can kill your mother too much. Or pretend that you killed her with disdain while depending on her domestic and emotional labour while confined to the same household. (If I were dictator, Montenegrin children would leave their families at majority age. Socio-economic conditions are less favourable to this everywhere around the world A.D. 2022, alas.)

The arts and culture could not imagine a way out of patriarchy, either. Oddly, there were no women novelists in Montenegro for the longest time, although there were many women poets. The Montenegrin novel only properly emerged in the communist era after the Second World War, when Montenegro for the first time in its history got to have a stable middle class. Serbia and Croatia had it earlier, by the mid-nineteenth century, and had the novel earlier, too.

Poetry ruled the day for centuries; Montenegro's prince-bishops wrote poetry. The folk poetry was transmitted orally, sometimes by illiterate, usually elderly, male storytellers. (Harvard scholars Milman Parry and Albert Lord visited Yugoslavia in the 1930s and 1950s respectively, studied the local oral poetry tradition and put forward a theory that that's how Homer's *Iliad* and *Odyssey* came to be: the Homeric recurring formulas in pre-set meter come from its original orality.) After the fall of the Byzantium and the South Slav principalities in the region, a small state of Zeta existed for some centuries (before the Ottoman empire conquered the entire area) and was one of the first places to try out the newfangled thing called the printing press, in 1493. Around this time, Zeta became more widely known as Montenegro. "Three factors explain the Ottoman failure to subdue it completely," according to Britannica: "The obdurate resistance of the population, the inhospitable character of the terrain (in which it was said that 'a small army is beaten, a large one dies of starvation'), and the adroit use of diplomatic ties with Venice." From the early 1500s on, Montenegro, run by that time by prince-bishops, carved itself out of the Ottoman empire and fought its way into statehood, first with a recognition from the Ottoman Porte in 1799, and then by an international treaty at the Berlin congress in 1878, its territory doubled and access to the sea finally secured, at today's Bar and Ulcinj. (I am skipping over many wars in between these dates.)

In short, it was a country of metered spoken poetry, and poetry maintained its political weight till well into the end of the communist era and the time of the inter-Balkan wars of the 1990s. The decasyllabic folk poetry from the time of the wars against the Ottoman empire and contemporary poetry that echoed it, formally or thematically, has been used as a tool of nationalist division. For the Serbs in Bosnia and Serbia, the largely secular Muslim minority in Bosnia-Herzegovina was now the equivalent or offspring of the old Turkish enemy. Montenegro was implicated by its alliance with Serbia, which it stuck with until after the wars of the 1990s ended. TV propaganda, of course, was a more important agent of change, and popular music, as well, but poetry was not innocent. While Ireland had a number of poets of reconciliation during the Troubles, poetry had become the most reactionary of art forms in the Western Balkans in the nineties.

I've sped too far ahead. It is in the post-Second World War era that Montenegro finally got its novels, with Mihailo Lalić and Čedo Vuković. But there were new obstacles on the horizon: the lure of Belgrade and other large cities. Ambitious Montenegrins with strong ties to the ruling communists would move to Belgrade, the capital of the newly-created federal Yugoslavia. The first governing establishment of the new country, heavily drawn from the partisans who fought Nazi occupation of the country, had a somewhat disproportionate number of Montenegrins from the get-go. There were many Montenegrins in top-level state security jobs and policing, and in other spheres, including culture. As the new Yugoslavia developed and built institutions, Montenegrins grew accustomed to being aware of the possibility of a parallel, more eventful life elsewhere, in the vast neighbouring republic of Serbia which already had an extensive middle class and a large capital city. While the communist rulers certainly invested in the industrial modernization of Montenegro, they lost interest in the arts, culture and post-secondary education. There was some theatre life, not a lot (playwrights tended to move to Belgrade or Zagreb), no film industry (the state would open and close film production companies according to its own inscrutable logic), and a patchy university system (for a good graduate degree, you had to go to Belgrade or Zagreb).

The result was a lost generation of Montenegrin creators, the sons and daughters of Montenegrin functionaries, who made up a considerable chunk of the new Belgrade middle class. There was the novelist Biljana Jovanović, daughter of Batrić Jovanović, whose intense, bold novels provoked and surprised before she died at a cruelly young age (her *Dogs and Others* has recently been translated to English). Or the daughter of Danica and Vojo Abramović, Marina, who describes her upbringing in a large, likely expropriated apartment in Belgrade with her high communist functionary mother in her recent biography *Walk Through Walls*. The partisans fought for a better future in all kinds of weather and harsh terrain, with only basic materiel, and then watched their children, raised in comfortable apartments, grow into softies: artists, novelists, rebellious and dependant at the same time. And they all became Serbs, their art part of Serbian art, their novels part of Serbian literature. (Probably the best-known Croatian writer for English-language readers today, the late Daša Drndić, grew up in Belgrade. Her father, leader of the anti-fascist uprising in Istria, ended up a post-war functionary in the federal capital. Her first novel is very much of the 'comfortable, mildly rebellious youth from the capital' kind).

In my own extended family, on my father's side, there is a Belgrade branch with one pater familias who worked in the secret service and lived in a leafy part of Belgrade in a pretty apartment, and whose children are confidently middle-class and urban. These very distant relatives probably saw me as a poor relation from the provinces the few times I visited their home as a student in Belgrade.

The newest cohort of Montenegro novelists, people my (generation X) age and the millennials who followed, are indeed the first cohort physically located in Montenegro. But they (we?) have been busy distancing themselves from the geography and the *terroir* in their fiction, and what good is that in nation-building? To return to the question from the Canadian chapters of this book: how local and national should narrative arts be? Nation is a feeling worth having and keeping alive. There is a huge amount of pastiche in Montenegrin novels, of escapism, inter-textuality, American pop culture, forays into genre fiction, an inordinate amount of literary postmodernism and pointless jokiness from writers of my vintage. Many of the novelists worship and echo the Austrian Thomas Bernhard, whose anti-patriotism and anger can certainly feel like a desired antidote to the parochial, nationalist Balkans, but grows tiresome in book after book. Some sort of apocalypse takes place in at least three prominent Montenegrin novels recently; in short stories, there are zombies and vampires. Some of the novels do engage with Montenegro's here-and-now. A noir set in the present-day capital follows a murder investigation which leads the hapless librarian narrator to the decadent parties of the ruling elite where, in a typical noir manner, the police are revealed to be as corrupt as the criminal underground and the elite. (In its first print run it sold 20,000 copies.) In another recent novel, the minister of culture, an obedient careerist, gradually turns into an insect.

There are few women among the novelists, and little interest among the male novelists in creating or centering plausible female characters. If they exist, they are given brief air time, as an unimportant girlfriend in a story of male friendship, or a boringly perfect (therefore mostly off-page) spouse or co-worker. If they do receive air time, it will be as a monstrous mother figure that must be annihilated. "How come your first novel is a series of stylistic exercises on the topic of Marquis de Sade whipping a peasant woman?"I ask the poet and film critic I've stayed in touch with via Viber over the years. "Ah but don't forget, in one of them de Sade gets whipped too!" was the defence he mounted.

When did women begin existing in world literatures? Meaning: as characters worth putting literary work into, of potentially universal reader interest? When did women writers reach critical mass? In the English language it's been at least since Mary Wollstonecraft (and her daughter, Mary Shelley), Jane Austen, the Brontës, George Eliot, Louisa May Alcott, Lucy Maud Montgomery. France? Certainly from de Beauvoir and such contemporaries as Violette Leduc. As far back as Colette, Georges Sand? Many aristocratic women wrote in pre-revolutionary France, and some were revered, but were Madame de Staël in the eighteenth century and Madame de Sévigné in the seventeenth groundbreaking? Perhaps the problem is that no critical mass of women writers followed in their wake. Women have to keep pouring into cultural life, generation after generation, for the effect to be seen. Maybe francophones will correct me with a fuller, longer list.

Some literatures are still awaiting their women, and Montenegro's is among them. The civic sector in Montenegro has always had a number of fearless women with platinum integrity, for example Vanja Ćalović, who is the head of a major anti-corruption NGO, and Ljiljana Raičević, the director of a shelter for women fleeing domestic violence. But electoral politics and public life in general have harboured extremely few with comparable influence. They must burst into the novel, and onto the agora. It's about time. When Montenegrin novelists allow novels to be the airy, multi-perspective, democratic forms that they can be, their novels will have more women. And politics will follow.

Chapter 10

THIS IS THE STORY OF how a Montenegrin novel set in 1943 with a connection to my great-uncle brought Northrop Frye into my life.

Mihailo Lalić (1914–1992) was a Montenegrin writer and Second World War veteran. *Hajka* (*The Chase*) is a novel that ends a quartet of books about a group of people in northern Montenegro in the early years of the Italian and German occupation and their part in a popular uprising which, after initial success, was brutally suppressed. (Later in the war, the partisans form an army, advance by liberating region after region and begin receiving international recognition and material support, but Lalić is interested in the much bleaker early period.)

A woman, Neda, sets out on foot in search of her lover who is part of a partisan guerrilla formation. She doesn't find him, but instead assumes her own stray storyline. The partisans come out of a dugout, fight for dear life, and most of them are killed. There are considerable losses on the other side, too. The northern Montenegro peaks and valleys, covered in snow, make everything grimmer. That, in broad strokes, is the novel.

The story-telling rings with tones of the Old Testament. The reasons why Neda leaves her in-laws' home, where she was mistreated and detested for suspected 'barrenness,' to look for her lover and warn him of a coming chase are told in one page of terse, fatalistic prose. Lalić runs through local events in northern Montenegro under Italian occupying forces as if there is no time to pause for sentiment. The Italian retaliatory shootings of civilians and captured partisans are described matter-of-factly. Džana, the mother of Neda's missing lover, takes a bullet for someone else; her unequivocal choices that led to that point take up the whole of two pages. Executed next to a steep-sided inlet of the river Lim, she turns her chair to face the firing squad. As a last wish, she is given two safety pins for her skirt, so it won't roll up and expose her body as she's falling down the cliff.

Hajka (the word means to chase, hunt, after a human being) opens in the free indirect speech of the first recurring character Paško Popović, a rambling village eccentric who carries a book on the lives of the saints everywhere he goes, and is given to philosophical pessimism. It is briefly mentioned that he was made a member (passive voice is accurate here) of the Italian militia as a sentry, a job he doesn't approach with dedication. He walks in and out of events throughout the book and is the first to run across the lost Neda, who keeps her intentions to herself. She is pregnant with her lover's child, and due to her advanced pregnancy she invites compassion rather than suspicion from the people she meets. Paško, Neda, and most of the other characters we get to know, including the communist partisans, are confounded by the magnitude of human cruelty. They contemplate the works of the Beast and demons in the world and the nature around them. There is an undercurrent of peasant Pagan-Christianity in the thinking of many partisans in the novel, in that of their local opponents, *chetniks*, and in the minds of the partisans' circumstantial allies, the faith leaders of the Muslim population. Demons sometimes speak through river waters, the hum of trees, the shrieks of birds, the pouring snow. But J.M. Coetzee knew this too: one doesn't need to be religious to admit to the existence of evil. Coetzee's alter, Elizabeth Costello, in *Elizabeth Costello* says that there is no better concept to name what humans sometimes do to humans and other life forms. There is no God, but evil, for which the monotheistic religions maintain naming rights, is not vacating any time soon.

I should pause here for a potted history of the inner Yugoslav wars during the Second World War. Europe was dividing itself into two military blocks in the late 1930s and the Kingdom of Yugoslavia signed the accession to the Axis powers in March 1941. It was not a popular decision, and the communist party, illegal for most of the kingdom's life, fired up the electorate's discontent with organized massive demonstrations. While "better war than the treaty" was heard on the streets, and "better grave than a slave," the British government's secret service helped deliver a pro-Allies military coup in the Yugoslav army. Hitler's Germany swiftly followed with a declaration of war on Yugoslavia and an all-out attack and occupation. Prince Regent Paul and the royal family escaped to Britain and the Yugoslav government's efforts towards the rapprochement with Germany came to naught. (Prince Paul features as a friend, possibly a lover, of the UK Conservative politician and socialite Sir Henry 'Chips' Channon in the first uncensored edition of Channon's 1918-1938 diaries which Penguin published in 2020.)

The Axis countries partition Yugoslavia, with Montenegro going to Italy. An uprising of the local population against the occupiers was largely organized by the communist party, which built cross-region alliances, educated (sometimes indoctrinated) people, raised class consciousness, admitted women to its ranks, and maintained connections with the Soviet Union (until 1948 and the famous breakup), all while developing a vision of a decentralized but unified communist Yugoslavia. Meanwhile, local Quisling troops were also formed, such as the Ustashe in Croatia. Other guerrillas formed and roamed the region. Chetniks came from peasant and lower middle-class stock and were fiercely anti-communist and ethno-nationalist, which landed them—sometimes circumstantially, often by conscious choice—on the side of the Italian and German occupiers.

After the end of communist Yugoslavia, a newly revived Serbian nationalism had its own historians who argued that the Chetniks never collaborated: they fought for *srpstvo* and Christian Orthodoxy, and anything to the contrary they insist was partisan propaganda. In Serbian public debates of the last decade, a line is often drawn from the Serbian royal family to the populist anti-communist parties and politicians and the Chetniks and further on to the Serbian wars of expansion of 1990s. What about the Chetnik massacres of the Muslims? ask the Muslim historians. What about Montenegrins: are they merely a side-note to the Serbian story, with no history of their own? This is an ongoing conversation in Serb nationalist circles that today dominate Serbian public life, and it keeps spilling over to Montenegro and Bosnia-Herzegovina, each with significant Serbian minorities. Those of us who don't believe in the manifest destiny of the march of Serbian nationhood in the wider Balkans see and live a very different history, national and global. (Yes, Croats have their own madness, but it's not nearly as regionally expansionist.)

Northern Montenegro has a considerable Muslim population, which added another battlefield to the Yugoslav civil wars in the 1940s. Some Muslims were neutral, some took the occupier's side, and some helped the partisans. The partisan-Chetnik divide ran not only between families of the same village or city, but within families. The fact that Churchill and the British government eventually recognized Tito's communist para-state structure as the official new Yugoslavia—and not whatever infrastructure the royalist Chetnik leaders had going in 1944—was a major thorn in the side of Serbian nationalist historians in the 1990s. (Michael Ondaatje uses the decision by the British to recognize Tito's communists as *the* Yugoslavia as a crucial plot point in his novel *Warlight*.)

Where were the South Slav liberal democrats while the communists were liberating the country, and national-populists were fighting the communists? Well. Otherwise engaged, I suppose. In Milovan Djilas's memoir *Rise and Fall* there is a chapter mulling over the fact that the two most prominent writers in the new Yugoslavia, Miroslav Krleža and the Nobel-winning Ivo Andrić, lay low during the war. Partisans had signalled Krleža, who was a communist intellectual in the kingdom of Yugoslavia, that they were waiting for him to join, but the signals went unheeded. As one of a handful of powerful men in the new country, Djilas interacted with both authors on multiple occasions and pondered the issue of Krleža and the partisans. When Djilas was condemned and ostracized for his critical writing, becoming probably the best-known dissident in Europe at that time, neither man came to his defence. Andrić was not brave, writes Djilas. And Krleža once said to a mutual friend that he could not join in the partisan liberation because he could not leave his wife and expose her to reprisals (nor could he have taken her with him). Djilas does not comment on that statement.

It wasn't only the liberals who kept low profiles. Other Communist parties around Europe were MIA, too. "Here, look: Bulgarians, for example, bragged endlessly, gave the world Dimitrov, had half of the population behind them, looked like they could do anything they wish— and did nothing, left the state apparatus intact, let it collaborate with the Axis, serve, carry," one of the partisans in the novel *Hajka* muses. "Hungarians had experience, their own revolution and military experts in Spain—they too are keeping quiet. Czechs had their own voters and MPs, the strongest party in the country—not a peep now. Italians too had something; it's obvious they did; all of their soldiers know and like to sing workers' songs, but what's the use when they'll only dare sing them when we disarm them and rescue them from their officers and fascists? Germans too had their fighters; they should still have them now, except they don't. Others had them too, but nobody moves [. . .] Looks like the beast in boots used some kind of poison to lull to sleep all those forces, and so lulled, killed them off. Only here that poison didn't work—but why? If we are insane, like the other side says we are—how did we survive the last two years? If we are not insane, like we believe, but resilient and resistant to poison—why has nobody joined us? Had anybody joined us—it would have set the world on fire, we would stand shoulder to shoulder, it would have been even more beautiful than the European Spring of 1848 . . ."

Hajka, like other Lalić novels set in wartime, takes place in the Northern Montenegrin mesh of partisans, Chetniks, Muslims, Italians, and the Italian-appointed local police. A group of partisans are spending the night in two separate dugouts, in hiding from an expected Italian and Chetnik search party. Some among them are impatient and—instead of hunkering down for the winter—initiate acts of sabotage: toppling electricity towers, bombing bridges. A hunt for their heads is in progress. A fresh layer of snow has covered the ground and made it impossible to move without leaving tracks. A few partisans are able to sleep. The rest listen to the water dripping and the damp cold seeping. Each person's background is presented through an inner monologue in this hour of the wolf. Neda, without knowing, comes close to one of the dugouts but is discovered by the Chetniks and presumed a lost simpleton. She is sent out of the way, to the house of one of the Chetnik leaders, where his mother and young daughters live. (The Chetnik leader's inability to make sons is a source of some resentment, we discover when the novel dips into his thoughts.) As the novel progresses, the *hajka* comes closer, the dugouts spill their contents, and the battles begin. As if out of spite, a magnificent sunny day dawns and the rays against the immaculate carpet of snow blind everyone to tears. All parties are on the move through desolate terrain electrified by light. Bullets bite like wasps or snakes (those, that is, that you survive to describe). The partisans are going through a Schubert *Winterreise* of sorts, each marching to his own demise, surrounded by apparitions of his pre-war life. A wounded partisan soldier, as his consciousness seeps away, is back in school, witnessing his baby sister being mocked for her clothes. "Whoever among us passes through here—it'll be easier after. Those who pass—they'll stop the bastards: from mocking the poor and sending *hajkas* after people. Life will be better after, and everyone will be dressed for weather—and no snakes in sight." Lado Tajović, the man that Neda has been looking for, and a recurring character in Lalić's novels, pales among other, more vivid characters of *Hajka*. He remembers her often, but as a persistent regret.

Had *Hajka* ever been translated into English, readers may have found the content unfamiliar, but the style and the tone recall Flannery O'Connor, the world of Southern Gothic, *The Road* by Cormac McCarthy, Marilyn Robinson's Protestantism-informed novels and, absolutely, John Steinbeck. While Lalić was a communist, his fiction and the world of his characters does not fully blossom into high modernism (although indeed the relentlessly walking and endlessly waiting partisans are brothers of Vladimir and Estragon). Rather, his novel is more collective, more epic perhaps (as in the *Iliad*, we follow all the chief warriors), and mythical. Lalić has certainly read his Victor Hugo and Shakespeare ("Life is nothing special," a young partisan reassures himself, "it's being barked on by one chase dog after another, and the little nothing between two dreams"). The devil as a character and a force, however, was likelier to have come via Dostoevsky and Russian literature than any of the American Christian novelists.

All but two of the partisans we follow are killed. Each individual death is described in detail, sometimes poetically, sometimes like a prolonged horror. It transpires, in not very many words, that the battle we witness at the end of the chase, and the skirmishes and blown bridges that led to it, were meant to keep the regional Chetnik leaders busy in the region and away from Bosnia, where the main partisan front has recently opened. Mission accomplished, with two detachments of partisans decimated.

The leader of one of them, Ivan Vidrić, makes it almost till the end. We meet him early on, in the dugout, as the only partisan whose wife, Gara, has joined the resistance alongside her husband. This particular detachment therefore has one woman in its midst and will lose her by a single remote sniper shot shortly before it loses Vidrić himself. Some pages later, a remote machine gun changes direction and mows him down. "From the torn veins spurted jets of blood into the lit space. Heart propels them to the sun, earth to itself—from their crossed arches between the snow and the sun, a red shrub appeared with flying red flowers." Vidrić sees it, and wonders: "where from, over my grave, such rain of flowers? . . ."

My mother and aunts have told me on many occasions that this character is based on their late uncle, Milan Kuč, whose spouse, Stana Crnga, also joined the partisans. They left behind a baby boy, as did Vidrić and Gara in the novel. (In one scene they quietly talk about their son, far away in safe hands.) Vidrić was killed on February 15, 1943, as was Milan Kuč (the novel is precise), at the age of thirty-three, while trying to break through the ring of Italian, Chetnik and Muslim militias surrounding a secret dugout. He too, like my great-uncle, was tasked by the communist party with keeping the illegal activities of education and mobilization alive after the bulk of partisan forces in Montenegro and Sandžak moved to Bosnia.

My mother's own father, the grandfather I never got to meet, was also killed as a partisan in a different operation when my mother was a toddler. As an idiot youth, I never inquired about the details, never asked to hear the whole story as she and my aunts remembered it. And since Lalić was mandatory reading in school (although not the bleak *Hajka*) I avoided his books, presuming them propagandistic. Why else would they be in the curriculum? Now that I'm interested, few people who can say anything of substance on the topic are still alive. One of my aunts kept in touch with the son who was a baby in 1943, but they eventually lost contact. He lives in Podgorica, I'm told. I doubt that he'd remember his parents even if I found him. Perhaps he has forgiven them for choosing history over parenting.

Then again, Lalić wrote fiction, and it's possible that almost everything in *Hajka* is fiction, or a merging of stories that Lalić had collected about and from people he had talked to in wartime and in peace. The impeccable, take-charge Vidrić appears in two preceding novels of the quartet, *The Evil Spring*, and *The Wailing Mountain*. Was all of that Milan Kuč? Last winter, I got in touch with Božena Jelušić, a literary critic in Montenegro, and (as of September 2020) an MP in the national assembly. She wrote the book of essays *The Mythical in Lalić's Novels*. I tell her, tentatively, because fiction is never documentary, that according to my family folklore, *Hajka* is about the death of my great-uncle. She reassures me that Lalić used oral histories and eye-witness accounts in his novels and made many people unhappy by preserving their acts in fiction. (After the war, he never returned to northern Montenegro, preferring instead to split his time between Belgrade and the Montenegrin coast.)

And here comes one of those improbable, magical connections between my two countries. What brought about Jelušić's book on Lalić was a new translation of Northrop Frye's *Anatomy of Criticism* in 2005, this time in Serbian (the earliest translation is from 1979, in the Croatian variant of the common language). She realized, she told me, the strength of the mythical element in Lalić, particularly after reading the third essay in *Anatomy*, 'Archetypal Criticism: Theory of Myths'.

"The four *mythoi* that we are dealing with," writes Frye in *Anatomy*, "comedy, romance, tragedy and irony, may now be seen as four aspects of a central unifying myth. *Agon* or conflict is the basis of archetypal theme of romance, the radical of romance being a sequence of marvellous adventures. *Pathos* or catastrophe, whether in triumph or in defeat, is the archetypal theme of tragedy. *Sparagmos*, or the sense that heroism and effective action are absent, disorganized or foredoomed to defeat, and that confusion and anarchy reign over the world, is the archetypal theme of irony and satire. *Anagnorisis*, or recognition of a newborn society rising in triumph around a still somewhat mysterious hero and his bride, is the archetypal theme of comedy." (P. 192)

To comedy, romance, tragedy, and irony correspond the seasons of spring, summer, autumn and winter, and Frye passes back and fourth through the centuries, starting with the Old and New Testaments and the Ancient Greeks and Romans, all the way to the early modernists in the latter half of the nineteenth century, establishing the connections of the expansive rhizome of western literature, with forays into music and painting. It's an exciting ride, as he explains the context and the resonances, the common *terroir*, of so many works.

Frye is out of fashion in Anglophone academia now and the reader who begins the 2000 reprint of *Anatomy* with the Harold Bloom foreword will quickly learn why. A kind of 'sociology of the text' literary method is popular now in criticism and literary conversations, in the media as much as in academe. Deconstruction made a ripple in the 1990s, but today it's hard to come across a critical exercise that does not ask questions about the pragmatics of the work: what does it do in the world, how is it being read and by what groups, did it help instill certain moral intuitions as natural, how does it resonate in the history of the human struggle for justice? The School of Resentment, according to Bloom (and his student Camille Paglia), will edge out literary criticism from universities, replacing it with cultural criticism. "The anatomies issuing from the academies concern themselves with the intricate secrets of Victorian women's underwear" and critical reading, the discipline of how to read and why, will survive in solitary scholars. "Such scholars, turning Frye's pages, will find copious precepts and examples to help sustain them in their solitude."

Of course, translated books don't transfer with them the fads, trends, and sociology of scholarship from their countries of origin, and while Jelušić is a feminist, she found Frye a sustaining proposition when faced with Lalić. Four of his best-known novels, she argues, *The Evil Spring*, *The Wailing Mountain*, *The Rupture*, and *Hajka*, are comfortably settled in Frye's spring, summer, autumn and winter scheme. A hero's journey through obstacles, *The Evil Spring*, is the story of a young student returning from a big city to his home town after the 1941 bombing of Belgrade and the Axis occupation of Yugoslavia, and his gradual realization that organized resistance is necessary, a "recognition of a newborn society rising." *The Wailing Mountain* follows the same man one year later, the first uprising suppressed and many of his peers dead. He is at a Gethsemane of sorts, with a handful of partisans left in Montenegro after the battleground has moved to Bosnia. All are worn down by loneliness and failing to see meaning in the continued fight against occupation. This is interrupted by a blooming romance: it is with Neda that he finds the path out of the Wailing Mountain, and they "once more saw the stars."

The Rupture, a tragic, autumnal novel, follows a side character from the previous novel who surrenders himself to the enemy. Over to Frye, writing about Milton's *Paradise Lost*: "As soon as Adam falls, he enters his own created life, which is also the order of nature as we know it. He enters the world in which existence is itself tragic . . . Merely to exist is to disturb the balance of nature. Every natural man is a Hegelian thesis, and implies a reaction: every new birth provokes the return of an avenging death. This fact, in itself ironic and now called Angst, becomes tragic when a sense of a lost and originally higher destiny is added to it." The role of the lost higher destiny in *The Rupture* is given to the revolution, which the protagonist begins to see as an impossible demand.

While *Hajka* indeed is wintry, I had some initial qualms about finding it in Frye's category that belongs to irony and satire. How, I wondered? Satire, he elaborates, is of the lighter stages of the category, while irony is a sister of darkness. Irony is what makes itself seen when we realize that "Hamlet dies in the middle of a frantically muddled effort at revenge which has taken eight lives instead of one." And darker still, it appears in the visions of *1984*, and Kafka's *In the Penal Colony*, both parodying religion and original sin: "Guilt is never to be doubted," Frye writes. The humans of this phase are "*desdichado* figures of misery or madness, often parodies of romantic roles . . . Sinister parental figures naturally abound, for this is the world of the ogre and the witch."

"But on the other side of this blasted world of repulsiveness and idiocy, a world without pity and without hope, satire begins again. At the bottom of Dante's hell, which is also the centre of the spherical earth, Dante sees Satan standing upright in the circle of ice, and as he cautiously follows Virgil over the hip and thigh of the evil giant, letting himself down by the tuffs of hair on his skin, he passes the centre and finds himself no longer going down but going up, climbing up on the other side of the world to see the stars again. From this point of view, the devil is no longer upright, but standing on his head, in the same attitude in which he was hurled downward from heaven upon the other side of the earth . . . Tragedy can take us no farther; but if we persevere with the *mythos* of irony and satire, we shall pass a dead centre, and finally see the gentlemanly Prince of Darkness bottom side up."

He would say that, Frye, Christian that he was. But Lalić wasn't one. There is very little redemption in the quartet of his wartime novels. It's a surprise that no communist Kulturträger objected to his pessimism. Lalić never wrote the novel of the Yugoslav liberation, and he died just as the country he fought for began to fall apart in a civil war, in 1992. His last novel, *Tamara*, is about partisans brutally disappearing one of their own during the war. Is it that surprising, the novel suggests, that their descendents who ran Yugoslavia ended up being no strangers to lies and theft? *Hajka* itself does not end with an overturned Prince of Darkness, but with Pashko, remembering Neda. "That woman that they lied to me comes from Medja, she's actually come from my church history book— she came out just so she could see if the world got better: she saw: it did not get better—people fight, rob, steal and chase others in *hajkas*. So she returned immediately to the dark, for nothing pains her in the dark. Nor does it pain Pashko—it's finally quiet: grass below, grass above him."

Chapter 11

YOU COULD ARGUE THAT Alice Munro's fiction is parochial. It wouldn't necessarily be a value judgment. A lot of the best literature is fiercely local and at the same time transcends its time and place to reach readers in other eras and locales. But before reading her closely, I was sure Munro's stories were parochial in that other sense: insular, uninterested in wide varieties of human experience, reiterative. After she won the Nobel Prize, amidst of a wave of excitement and praise, two dissenting voices stood out: novelist Lydia Millet and critic Christian Lorentzen both criticized what they saw as Munro's narrowness, bourgeois mindset, and exclusive attention to love and sex intrigues among the middle classes of small town Ontario. Why would we care about these people? A small-town Ontario woman having an affair, then leaving both her husband and lover to move across the country to small-town B.C. to open a bookstore. How is this interesting? Mavis Gallant, another Canadian short story writer beloved by *The New Yorker*—now she was worldly, with a well-travelled imagination, I thought. She lived in Paris, for heavens sake. (Snobbery will find each of us if we're not careful, and what is more parochial than snobbery?)

As the second decade of my life in Canada drew to a close, I found myself feeling less like I belonged than when my passport was first stamped at the Montreal Airport in 1999. Reasons are multiple. I have entered middle age, and like the narrator of Aleksandar Hemon's most recent book, *My Parents / This Does Not Belong To You*, I began to track the line of decisions that led here, and wonder if they were correct. By my twentieth year in Canada, I have met my walls and can guess where the locked doors are, while ten or fifteen years ago, early in my citizenship, I presumed that all was open, the possibilities endless. I also did not want a hyphen to my citizenship, and Montenegrin-Canadian sounds a drag to say, let alone imagine. I had no children in local school. No institutional affiliation. Was I really Canadian?

Against this background, I came across the two stories by Alice Munro touching on Montenegro. The country where I spent my first eighteen years, where almost all of my remaining family live, is the least known and smallest of the post-Yugoslav countries of the western Balkans. People usually have some notion of Serbia, Croatia, and Bosnia, but not of Montenegro. And yet, here it is, in the work of Alice Munro, who can have her pick of small and unusual countries for fictional purposes. I've had the Penguin anthology of her *Selected Stories* on a shelf somewhere for a long time, but I've only recently read the "Albanian Virgin." The other story of interest, "Tricks," appeared in the collection *Runaway*.

"Tricks" opens as Robin, a young woman in a small Ontario town, is getting ready to travel to Stratford for a theatre matinee. Her sister and neighbour are playing cards and are wondering what the fuss is about: her green dress will surely arrive from the dry cleaner on time. Robin is a nurse and her sister has health problems and we presume lives with her because she requires care. The reader gradually finds out that this is a repeat trip to Stratford for Robin. When she attended a matinee of *Antony and Cleopatra* last year, Robin lost the purse containing her documents, money, and train ticket back, and was stopped on the street by a stranger wondering if she was in distress. The stranger, whose name is Danilo Adžić, turns out to be from Montenegro, then still part of the larger Yugoslavia, but it's Montenegro that the author is interested in as Danilo's place of origin. He lives alone in Stratford and owns a clock repair shop. The young woman trusts him immediately and agrees to follow him home so he can lend her some money and make dinner for them both. Robin has never had a boyfriend, but she's something of a fantasist and Danilo strikes her as a pleasant stranger. She ponders the rescued-by-a-handsome-stranger narrative as if she were a character in a story and doesn't entirely discard it. We trust Danilo alongside her, he is reliable somehow.

The conversation proceeds in skipped-over impasses. "What are you famous for, then" asks Robin after Danilo says that Montenegro is not famous for its food. He asks in turn, "And you?" whereupon she regrets putting her question in those terms. (I've never tried that response, personally. For me, it goes, "You wouldn't happen to know of the tennis player Miloš Raonić? No, he was some time ago. The operetta *The Merry Widow*? There was this American indie film screened at TIFF a couple of years ago, *Meet me in Montenegro*? . . . Alright, never mind, let's move on.") We learn that Danilo is to return to Montenegro to deal with a family matter and that he probably won't be back before June the next year. At the train station they kiss (you can almost hear violins as the melodrama heightens for Robin), and she promises that she'll meet his request to knock on his door in the same green dress on the same day next year, after her matinee of choice.

Robin spends the intervening year learning about Montenegro, to place Danilo in a context and give him a past. When the story returns to the present, Robin's green dress is still not ready and she ends up buying a similar one, with a more 'modern' cut. The play she's seeing in Stratford is *As You Like It*, in which Rosalind, disguised as a man, seeks her stray fiancé in the magic forest of Arden. When Robin finally knocks on Danilo's door after the play, he interrupts his work, opens the door in irritation, waves his hand at her and slams the door.

The first heartbreak is a rite of passage, the first locked door on a personal geography. Seasons move from summer to winter, and we find Robin forty years later, the capable chief nurse of a psychiatric ward in her home town, living alone (her sister has died), a string of affairs but no long relationship behind her. A lot of Munro's characters are women outside the marital formula: the never-married, those who regret getting married, the leavers, the abandoned, the widows. What kind of a Munro story would a happy couple make, and would they come across as obnoxious as Tom and Jerry do in Mike Leigh's *Another Year?* Munro, age 90 as I write this, is of a generation in which unmarried women read as somewhat eccentric (as they still do in most of the world). But they are 'centric' for Munro, the centre of the story. When a group of patients on their way to another hospital are temporarily placed on Robin's ward, she spots a man, weak, unable to speak. But surely, she thinks, Danilo? "Aleksandar Adžić", says the chart, born in Montenegro, Yugoslavia, emigrated May 29, 1962, care of brother Danilo Adžić (in this way we learn that Robin and Danilo met in 1961), lived with his brother until the latter's death in 1995. Deaf-mute from birth . . . apathy, mood swings, no training in sign language.

"This is ridiculous. This I do not accept." Twins! Danilo must have stepped out for an errand before she knocked on his door, she thinks.

It's one of those events that are too absurd for fiction, but not for real life. Writes Munro: "Shakespeare should have prepared her. Twins are often the reason for mix-ups and disasters in Shakespeare. A means to an end, those tricks are supposed to be. And in the end the mysteries are

solved, the pranks are forgiven, true love or something like it is rekindled."
This is followed by a darker wave of musing. Their relationship, had they
connected, would have been hard to maintain. How could they have
lived together, each with a dependent in tow? Perhaps it is better like this,
Robin tentatively thinks: better a brutal cut than a protracted cooling off.
"Robin has had patients who think that combs and toothbrushes must
lie in the right order, shoes must face in the right direction, steps must be
counted, or some sort of punishment will follow." Perhaps, if she follows
that worldview, her choosing the wrong kind of green dress put things in
motion in the wrong way.

What is inevitable and what contingent, what is imposed on us
and what have we chosen for ourselves? Alice Munro's fiction keeps
returning to these questions. Hers are often characters—women—who
fear freedom, or rush too carelessly into the first opportunity that gives
the illusion of freedom. Some manage to be free at great expense. In
"Albanian Virgin", Munro creates an Edwardian lady traveller (similar
to real life anthropologist Edith Durham) who comes from Canada, then
still part of the British Empire, to explore the Balkans. Her parents are
dead, and she's had a falling-out with her brother, so nobody back home
misses her much. The steamer from Trieste makes an overnight stop
in Bar, Montenegro, where she would like to stay longer. But Mr. and
Mrs. Cozzens, whom she met in Italy, and an English gentleman they've
introduced her to will "make a fuss" if she's not back on the boat in the
morning. She gets up early, asks for a guide at the hotel reception, and
goes on what she believes will be a short hike. They don't make it far
before her guide is killed, in a blood feud, she learns later. She herself is
wounded and taken as unexpected bounty to a tribe in northern Albania.
The only way to escape the marriage that the tribe arranges for her, she's
told by the Italian-speaking Franciscan who roams the local villages, is

to become a sworn virgin, taking a vow of chastity and wearing male clothing. So she does: she cuts her hair, dons men's clothes, and moves further up the mountain to live a solitary life. She leads her herd of sheep out to pasture and collects the milk that is taken back to the tribe. With winter on the horizon, the Franciscan hears rumours anew of an arranged marriage for the foreign woman and urges her to escape by following him to Skodra, the closest town. They eventually get there on foot, and find the bishop's house and the British consulate. Before she sets off on a boat to Italy, she will have to relearn to express her thoughts in English, sit on a chair, and eat with fork and knife.

However, the narration is not that straightforward: the story of the Canadian sworn virgin is actually told to the narrator, a bookshop owner in Victoria who has just moved from small-town Ontario (of course) after a marriage-ending affair, leaving both her husband and lover behind. Her eccentric, this-time-married acquaintance, Charlotte, is actually telling the story from her hospital bed, as an "idea for a film." Parallel to the Montenegrin-Albanian goings-on, the narrator is revealing her inner life and recent past. Charlotte survives the hospital stay, but the two women lose touch over the next couple of years. What would the marriage with her lover have been like, the narrator wonders, had she stayed with him? "We become distant, close—distant, close—over and over again," but they "get over all this."

It's never entirely clear how we're to connect the three protagonists of the story, the Ontarian bookshop owner in Victoria, the ailing then disappearing Charlotte, and Lottar, the Edith Durham figure. I'm not sure if we should try. Both the heroic and the deadly dangerous aspect of women's lives in wealthy democratic societies have diminished so much today that we seek fulfilment by taking on lovers and opening shops—is that what Munro means? Looking at the changing city of Victoria, the narrator wonders, "Views and streets deny knowledge of us, the air grows thin. Wouldn't we rather have a destiny to submit to, then, something that claims us, anything, instead of such flimsy choices, arbitrary days?"

This could have been uttered in Toronto of 2021, from my fifteenth-floor rental *kula* on Upper Jarvis. Sworn virgins still exist in remotest Albania, the last generation of them captured in photographs and documentaries, and Montenegro used to have them. (When the last one passed away not long ago, Montenegro's national broadcaster marked the occasion). It occurred to me, while in the company of Alice Munro, that my life now isn't that different from theirs back then: they herded sheep; I herd words, and do part-time jobs that let me herd words the rest of the time. They've forsaken the marital heterosexual formula and children so they can be freer, and so have I. Perhaps my ancestors have caught up with me, however far I've tried to escape?

To Montenegro, Munro attributes a kind of mystery. It's an incomprehensible yet oddly inviting place, somewhere to yearn for. A place of perennial yearning. As the global pandemic has made travel difficult, it's been almost two years since my last visit and I have no idea when I will be able to return. For the first time, I have an inkling of what it's like to miss Montenegro as an entity. For Lottar, the Canadian travelling in the Balkans, Montenegro is a place that she desires but is prevented from experiencing. "She would never take the road over the mountains to Cetinje, Montenegro's capital city—they had been told that it was not wise. She would never see the bell tower where the heads of Turks used to hang, or the plane tree under which the Poet-Prince held audience with the people. She could not get back to sleep, so she decided . . . to go a little way up the road behind the town, just to see the ruins that she knew were there, among the olive trees, and the Austrian fortress on its rock and the dark face of Mount Lovćen."

The question of whether I belong in Canada remains to be settled. What is clear, however, is that a place exists for me in Alice Munro's stories.

Chapter 12

S O MANY MEDIA DISAPPEARED in the last decade. In Toronto, the print edition of the *Daily Extra* is gone, and its online magazine abandoned all in-depth writing about arts and literature, focusing on pop culture instead. The weekend edition of *Corriere Canadese, Tandem*, which dedicated entire pages to opera, is over and out. *Macleans* doesn't cover arts and ideas any more. Alternative weeklies are kaput, first the *Eye/Grid*, then *Now*. TorStar purchased from Post Media and then retired Toronto's free subway paper, *Metro*. The *Star* itself abandoned arts coverage, abolished critics, cut ties with its entertainment permalancers. Before that, the *National Post* and the *Sun* did the same. As of writing, the other national daily, the *Globe and Mail*, maintains a threadbare arts and books coverage. Its theatre critic is the last one standing, the only one enjoying full-time employment in the whole of Anglophone Canada.

The US outlets that gave me a foothold in American cultural writing—*The Awl* and *The Believer*—are also gone. *Listen* abandoned print and is now a Steinway-owned website. Other outlets have emerged, as the US media market is continuously shape-shifting. *ArcDigital* became an important forum for diversity of opinion in 2020 and then radically cut its budget. The Berlin-based American-German *Van*, perhaps the future of classical music digital magazines, remains burdened by a similarly modest freelance budget.

American dailies have been dropping art criticism as well, but the situation is nowhere near as bad as in Canada: the *NYT* is actually increasing arts coverage and building a global readership for it; the Amazon-owned *Washington Post* holds on to its Arts & Entertainment section; the *San Francisco Chronicle* and the *Chicago Tribune* keep the A&E sections alive with a mixture of wire copy, local theatre and music stories, and global entertainment news. Who will still cover the live arts, apart from the *Times*, in ten years' time? My subscriptions meanwhile have been moving to Substack newsletters, podcasts, and British magazines.

Should a culturally curious tourist land in Canada in 2022 and open a daily paper or turn to the national broadcaster, she will conclude that Canada has little in the way of live arts and no national culture. In the latter half of the 2010s in Canada, the people running dailies, magazines, and the national broadcaster have each in their own way, possibly using different internet traffic analytics, come to the conclusion that they should get out of the business of arts criticism and in-depth coverage of culture and ideas, and quit investing in new generations of journalists who will be capable of introducing a vastly diverse readership to major questions in philosophy, literature, dance, or opera. It has all been deemed dispensable, a perhaps regrettable but nonetheless acceptable loss in the clunky transfer from print to digital that each medium has undergone. While the pains of this transfer and the loss of advertising to Google and Facebook are acute around the Anglophone world, the loss of arts coverage has been Canada's own phenomenon.

Another changing aspect of art criticism in Canada, one that is probably connected to economic scarcity, is the tearing down of barriers between criticism and political activism. Perhaps it was the pandemic shutdown of the nation's entire culture, except for the production of online content, that sped up what was already on the horizon. The tabulating of ethnicities in an artistic creation, figuring out who is allowed to say what on which topic by virtue of their identity, has overtaken the Canadian art conversation and is here to stay. Granted, similar issues are demanding centre stage in the UK and the US, in both commercial and elite arts, but they are far from dominating all conversations, as they do in Canada.

I have complained in earlier chapters of this book that Canadians, eager consumers of American culture, don't see themselves as a people connected by a national culture. If we ever have, we certainly do not now. Canadian mainstream media's near complete withdrawal from Canadian cultural production outside TV and film has helped us reach that state. There have been other factors. For instance, the weakening of arts education in public schools, which produces cross-generational gaps in audience and readership. A lot of advanced art training, especially in operatic singing, conducting, and visual arts, is now the exclusive domain of upper-middle-class children, because they require straight-up investment until well after the post-graduate level. Costly MFA programs likewise limit the production of fiction and long form nonfiction to elites. The consumer markets that enable Canadian novelists, mezzo-sopranos, choreographers, pianists, and sculptors to make a living (or two-thirds, or half a living) from their work are shrinking. The gutting of affordable housing in the federal austerity budget of 1995, the subsequent provincial off-loading of housing subsidies to the municipal level, and the role of capital in the extreme rise of home ownership costs and renting in the largest cities of Anglophone Canada have all played their part. Toronto's city hall allowed the condominium boom without asking much from developers in the way of creating new venues for performing arts or civic centres. (Ask any of the theatre veterans still living south of Steeles about the state of Toronto's theatre buildings, but only if you have some time.)

Much of the arts and culture that will be made in the near future will go unnoticed. We should be aware of that. What will be noticed by the media is most likely to be noticed for non-artistic reasons: perceived ideological faux pas, insufficient commitment to the political issue du jour, insensitive comedy, offensive or insufficient representation, young employee rebellions and leaks, all kinds of #metoo and para-#metoo callouts. The arts funding bodies on all three levels will, I expect, continue to change the funding eligibility criteria from the now embarrassing term 'excellence' to values such as representation, relevance, reconciliation, decolonization, *queering* (a word that means everything and nothing these days), community, respect, healing, equity.

In the years ahead, I will have to turn to writing about tech, or food and food production, or nature and wilderness, and, more importantly, open and free conversations about anything and everything of concern for a functioning society, without taboos and censure. I would like to write about comedy and take it seriously as an art form, but I expect comedy will go the way of the arts.

I find myself trying to embrace a culture that seems to be dissipating.

* * *

Media in the western Balkans have their own recurring challenges, only some of which are due to economic upheavals similar to what the internet did to print media in high-income countries. I caught the magazine bug at the early age of eleven, when I discovered the bi-weekly *Svijet* (*The World*) which was printed in Zagreb. It was technically a women's magazine; it contained the obligatory sections for recipes, style, and serialized women-centred fiction, but it was also an open-minded, leftist but high-brow, internationally-focused, second-wave feminist magazine (Gloria Steinem was an occasional contributor in the late 1980s), with long form articles on arts and culture. It had contributors with a penchant for Proust and Balzac. It would send a correspondent to the Venice Film Festival and she'd bring back interviews with rising indie music creator Laurie Anderson and first-time filmmaker Patricia Rozema. It's where I first heard of Patricia Highsmith, after her novel *Edith's Diary* was translated for the local markets, and while I was too young to read it then, the description of it stuck with me until I finally read it in Canada (it's a masterwork). It's where I first heard of Margaret Drabble, whose book, *The Millstone*, was serialized in the magazine. (I would get to meet and interview Margaret Drabble in 2013.)

The World did tell me about the world, and that writing about it is exciting and worthwhile. *The World* did not survive the end of communism and the region's transition to capitalism, and neither have its sister magazines from the same Zagreb-based company, the general interest *Start*, and the political weekly *Danas*. Yugoslavia fell apart, Croatia became its own country, I went to journalism school in Belgrade. I always leaf through the dozen *Svijet* and several Start issues that I still own and store in what used to be the children's bedroom in my late parents' apartment in Montenegro when I visit there. The last time I crossed the ocean, I brought with me to Toronto an issue which includes Slavenka Drakulić's interview with Kurt Vonnegut about the point of creative writing programs, and if it's possible to teach anybody to write.

Belgrade, when I lived there, was the Milošević-era Belgrade under international economic sanctions. Therefore, never a dull day, politically. In my fourth year, I was an intern at one of the few remaining independent media, the daily *Borba*, later called *Naša Borba*. Created after the Second World War to fulfill the role of possibly the most pro-regime daily in

Yugoslavia, *Borba* found its spine in the late eighties and positioned itself in favour of liberal-democratic values and against Milošević and the wars he was exporting to Serbia's neighbours. (It, too, perished on the rainbow bridge to capitalism, ceasing publication a few years after the NATO bombing of Serbia and Montenegro.) Occasionally, the city beat would send me on unglamorous reporting assignments nobody else would take, but often my pitches were taken seriously and accepted, especially for the spacious weekend edition. I wrote about the life of French philosopher Simone Weil, and a couple of weekends later conducted a Q&A with feminist philosopher Alison Jaggar, who happened to be in town. I'd poll translators and writers about books that they thought brought nothing but trouble to the humankind, and a week later I'd write about the Franciscan friars on the Montenegrin coast (a rare foray into writing about the place I was actually from). *Borba* wasn't the only outlet opposing the regime: there was a TV station, one or two radio stations, a newly created daily, and a magazine—all exceptions in the predominantly pro-Milošević media.

Paradoxically, there are fewer independent media today, after at least two major changes of government since Milošević, and under Serbia's democratically elected strongman Aleksandar Vučić. "The independent media survived dictatorship but they won't survive democracy," is how media and communications scholar Snježana Milivojević described the Serbian predicament. I called Dr. Milivojević, a professor of journalism and media studies at my alma mater, the University of Belgrade, Department of Political Science, and asked her about her prediction. In Milošević's time, she said, the West took interest in what was going on in the region, and the international agencies found ways to financially assist the few remaining anti-regime media outlets. On October 2000, Milošević was removed from power by the ballot box and, after his refusal to step down, by popular uprising. An era was presumed ended. Serbia, it was expected, would diversify its own media and see them through to the free marketplace.

Widespread commercialization followed. Foreign media ownership entered an already tightening print market and the stewardship of national flagship companies was not a priority for foreign owners (profit was). The commercial enterprise Pink TV, owned by a Serbian tycoon who thrived under Milošević, spread across the region its diet of reality shows, soaps from Turkey, India, and Latin America, and a bare minimum of news, usually slanted in favour of the ruling party. A new force on the scene, the daily tabloid papers, emerged to set an ethno-nationalist agenda for the rest of the media. They appeared in mysterious ownership patterns, forming and re-forming and disappearing based on shifts in the political climate or, as a report from the Helsinki Committee for Human Rights in Serbia put it, depending on whether or not an election was in the offing, or a political cause needed propping.". The tabloids that persist tend to be close to the ruling Serbian Progressive Party. The Russian government-owned news agency Sputnik is also present in Belgrade (at least two of the people from my journalism class of 1997 are employed there full-time), as is the US government-funded Radio Free Europe (another colleague from my class is the chief news editor). There is currently a single TV news channel that freely scrutinizes (and satirizes) the government: Nova, which has attracted a number of anti-regime media personalities from other outlets that lost their political independence. Serbian citizens are still buying print dailies and magazines. The habit has not yet disappeared. Nor is advertising entirely gone from print media. But neither circulation nor advertising is likely to grow with the omnipresence of the internet and the dominance of televisual media.

In Montenegro, things are slightly different. *Vijesti* used to be a small opposition daily. In the summer of 1999, just before leaving for Canada,

I wrote a series introducing feminist ideas for its culture section. The paper is now a company that includes a TV news channel and the highest circulation daily in the country. *Vijesti*'s four principal founders remain present in the ownership of the daily, while foreign co-investors changed: Westdeutsche Allgemeine Zeitung (WAZ) owned a 50 percent stake for a few years in the noughts, after which the US-based Media Development Investment Fund purchased 25 percent and an Austrian media group the other 25 percent. Arguably the best Montenegrin daily, *Vijesti* is now a mix: highly skilled, fair, and bold reporting, and often strongly partisan opinion. Although I grumble about the opinion and the clickbait and the owner's column (imagine Rupert Murdoch writing a highly irritable column about electoral politics in the *Times* for two decades), I visit its website daily and subscribe to the You Tube channel where I can watch its political talk shows. Unlike much of Canadian, US or UK television, substantial, wide-ranging and confrontational live TV interviews with political figures, often veering into historical discussion, still exist on the two privately-owned channels available in Montenegro, TV Vijesti and A1. While politicians of Margaret Thatcher's generation made themselves available for adversarial interviews and considered it part of the job, that is no longer the case in the UK or Canada. A new generation of leaders rely instead on public relations advisors. Perhaps these leaders lack mettle. Or perhaps they're conceding that internet bubbles have changed the public conversation in all media. This withdrawal from confrontational interviews so far has been slow in coming to continental Europe. How do countries with deep democratic traditions and incomparable wealth fare worse at holding leaders accountable than a young democratic, post-communist state? It's difficult to square. But here's to substantial TV interviewing and its contributions to responsible government.

Another well read daily, *Dan*, has remained steadfast in its pro-Serbian nationalist stance over the years. It has been as critical of the thirty-year-ensconced regime as *Vijesti*, but from a very different angle. A study by Daniela Brkić of the South East European Media Observatory notes that the publishing company that owns *Dan* was "funded with capital of dubious origin during the Slobodan Milošević's dictatorship," but has remained in the possession of two families all these years. In 2004, the paper's editor-in-chief Duško Jovanović was murdered in a drive-by shooting outside the *Dan* offices. It is widely presumed he was assassinated because of the paper's interest in ties between the country's political overground and the criminal underground. A person involved in the murder was tried, found guilty, and sentenced to nineteen years in prison, but where the order to assassinate came from and why remains unresolved.

Several other unsolved cases of assaults on journalists have led to Montenegro's ranking 104th on the Reporters Without Borders' World Press Freedom Index. (Serbian courts have had their own challenges persecuting assaults and murder of journalists.) *Vijesti*'s investigative reporter Olivera Lakić, who covers crime and corruption, was shot in the leg in 2018, presumably as a warning. The perpetrator was never found. The same journalist was beaten up several years earlier after reporting about cigarette smuggling operations. She had police protection for a time, but not long enough. In 2020, ahead of the general election on August 30, an anonymous website emerged declaring that two journalists from *Vijesti* and various opposition figures were "in the employ of the Serbian secret service." In 2015, an investigative journalist covering organized crime and war crimes, Jovo Martinović, was detained and held in pretrial detention for fourteen months. Despite insufficient evidence, he was charged with facilitating a meeting between drug dealers and buyers in a drug trafficking ring. Several professional associations pleaded his case, to no avail. In October 2020, Montenegro's high court sentenced him to a year in prison (which he had already served in detention). Martinović believes the charges were in retaliation for his reporting, and he is pursuing an appeal.

The oldest and least read daily, the state supported *Pobjeda*, is consistently pro-government, as are many popular online news portals and the national broadcaster, TVCG. Over the last three decades, TVCG has acquired scarcely any autonomy, despite many attempts and internal upheavals. The recent parliamentary majority has finally managed to appoint a new governing council which chose the new GM, so maybe this is about to change.

Words and writing matter in such a politically febrile society. Journalism can still be dangerous, rulebooks are still being written and, after the first change of government in a long while, ground will continue to shift. Six-hundred-thousand citizens is too small a market to sustain a wide variety of media through advertising and subscriptions: should foreign capital, tycoon capital, and public funds dry up, more media will be lost. Montenegro's problem is not the print and televisual hegemony of the *ancien regime* forces, as in Serbia, but the economic fragility of the current relatively diverse status quo, and the unpredictable judicial framework within which the media operate.

The long simmering problems of media freedom and diversity in Eastern Europe have become more acute of late. Western journalists are busy with their own funding and quality problems in the age of data analytics, social media, and disappearing advertising, but occasionally a foreign correspondent will spotlight the worsening situation in the East. In an August 2020 column, Hannah Lucinda Smith, the *London Times* correspondent based in Istanbul, compared the region to Turkey, which is more overtly dictatorial, and described Eastern Europe's press freedoms as nearing extinction: "[B]ehind the plethora of publications and channels on offer, a creeping monopolisation has wiped out almost all reporting that veers from the state-sanctioned line. Europe's illiberal governments no longer have to rely on *Pravda*-style outlets to control what people hear about . . . The new propaganda is privatised, subcontracted to cronies and inflated with cash." In Hungary, Bulgaria, Albania, Poland, and most of the former Yugoslavia, "businessmen are reaping fortunes by running mouthpieces." She documented some of the more blatant cases of conflict between fast profits and fair reporting, and the western Balkans were not even the worst of the bunch: the bigger headache for the EU and other multilateral bodies are Orban's Hungary; and Poland, which criminalized abortion. To quote a friend who works at Radio Free Europe, you can see where Europe has been going when we are not its worst problem any more.

It's been strange following the Eastern European situation from North America, where universities are in the process of deciding whether free inquiry is the highest value to strive for, or if there are more pressing goals for which that freedom should be curtailed. In Canada, as in the US, the media, too, are having second thoughts. Precedents of unpublished stories (because of backlash on social media) are slowly accruing. Public libraries are for the most part still holding steady, but expect organized protests if you book a room to discuss an unpopular cause. It's fairly easy to predict that a political scientist like Frances Widdowson, who argues from the position of the dialectic-materialist left in favour of one citizenship for all Canadians whether settler or indigenous, would now be an unwelcome and vocally-protested guest at the vast majority of Canadian universities and would rarely be heard in the media. The same can be said of any speaker who argues that we should keep sports separated according to sex (or else we'll see the end of women's sports) and against gender self-identification in general. The *Vancouver Sun*'s unpublishing of an Alberta researcher's op-ed proposing that Canadian society reconsider its annual six-digit immigration intake (quoting Robert Putnam's *E Pluribus Unum*) revealed another update on what's beyond-the-pale. Canadian media, traditional and social, and the university teaching profession joined in the public condemnation. Various foreign topics may get you de-platformed, unpublished, make you lose sponsors, or get you monstered on social media: reprinting the French or Danish Mohammed cartoons, singling out Israel for criticism, and, lately, in the US of all places, criticising the Chinese Communist Party. I expect the number of these will grow.

There are probably other until-recently-discussable topics that are coming close to being unsayable. Opposition to gay marriage, or support for Quebec's Laïcité law if you live in English-speaking Canada, perhaps. The weariness and rejection of all organized religion, yes including those other ones, too. Arguing that writers should be allowed to create characters of different ethnicities, and that non-matching actors should be allowed to play them. That we should not bury a work of art because of what its creator did in his or her private or political life. That the term 'cultural appropriation' is unhelpful and inaccurate. That, no, one will not put pronouns in the work email signature because one does not believe in the worldview of which they are a part, and refuses to pretend otherwise.

A *Harper's* magazine letter on justice and open debate, signed by a number of prominent writers, journalists, and editors in July 2020, kicked up a storm of criticism, chiefly from the left. The letter diagnosed the current situation as unwelcome and highly unusual for a liberal-democratic country, but it did not stem any tides. If anything, the situation has worsened. If there's a noisy group of complainants on social media (and sometimes a dozen voices is enough) assailing any institution over anything its writer or artist has said that the group judges harmful, hateful, and worse, bets can be placed on imminent firing and public apology. Print media, book publishing, and universities used to be understood as—by definition—the *loci* of free conversations and free examination of sources, but this consensus no longer holds. In other areas of human activity where the at-will employment contract has a tenuous relationship with employee free speech, on and off work hours, the situation is also worsening. The only reason Canada is lagging the US in writerly departures from mainstream outlets to Substack, podcasting, or forced early retirement is that paying media jobs are fewer here after years of closures and cost-cutting.

Offense archaeology, the digging out of old statements or writings for the purposes of public criticism in the present, is booming on both sides of the border. Coordinated mass reporting of allegedly 'hateful' content or tweets can not only get a user banned but a blog post removed from WordPress or Medium. Often these decisions are left to the algorithm because hiring and training human content moderators for the extraordinary number of online interactions taking place every minute is next to impossible.

Yes, there are economic causes behind all this frenzy. The media industry is in radical transformation (some would argue decline), its management skittish and unable to see the forest for the trees; traditional (i.e. non-coding) writing and journalism jobs are fewer than in the past, and the scramble for them is more ferocious than ever. As more print media move to the subscription model, which depends on traffic, it will become obvious that the business plan is not far removed from crowd-funding: the subscribers can and do cancel for political reasons and can hold the medium captive by demanding its ideological allegiances be respected.

But not all the problems are economic. The public inter-staff denunciations in major papers and public letters demanding the firing or re-education of colleagues are new. To me, they have a Soviet flair, yet we've read such letters from a section of *The Guardian's* US staff against one of the paper's columnists, from *New York Times's* staffers against the paper's science reporter, and from employees of the *Toronto Star* against a columnist's email message to management. It was not the economic pressure of holding precarious jobs that prompted the *Star* letter. Some, if not most of the writers signing these letters to management, like those demanding that libraries ban a radical feminist writer and blogger from renting a room on its premises, actually believe that restricting chunks of mainstream speech is a pressing and worthy cause. When writers and journalists take up against open inquiry and discussion, a significant change has taken place in the polity.

I, who dreamed of liberal democracies from within illiberal societies, believed that liberties based on ideals of fairness and equality before the law, once gained, were permanent. I was foolish. Those ideals and liberties only survive if there are people willing to uphold them and practice them, even when circumstances harden, even at personal inconvenience, and sometimes at the cost of gigs, jobs, and friendships. As George Packer eloquently said on receiving the Christopher Hitchens Prize, writers shouldn't be in this business for popularity and belonging; they must be prepared to go it absolutely alone if their conscience demands it.

By moving to Canada, I thought I would finally achieve a private life sheltered from the march of weighty political problems. I would dedicate myself to my wild orchids (including opera, mezzo sopranos, Monteverdi, Mozart, Mahler, Virginia Woolf, experimental fiction, abstract painting, lesbians on film, cycling in Paris, dabbling in fiction in my adopted first language.) But no life is all wild orchids, not even in liberal democracies, which are works in progress anyway. Having left a political culture where freedom of speech needs defending, I find myself in another political culture where freedom of speech needs defending. It's bizarre, but I know there are worse fates. And anyway, it'll be an honour.

Chapter 13

GREY STONES OF THE Dalhousie Arts and Administration Building under blue skies. Attic room under slanted roof at Shirreff Hall. Creaky floors of the philosophy department. Flaming foliage of autumn. Sitting next to a window on the top floor of Killam Library with the sun coming in, listening to the voice of Glenda Jackson as Inez in an LP recording of Sartre's *No Exit*, noticing the water of Northwest Arm. Cherry pie rectangles in the café on Coburg. First swim in Williams Lake. Victorian-dressed carollers inside the administration building. Adèle Hugo's letters to her unrequited obsession, an officer of the British army stationed in Halifax, kept in the Nova Scotia Archives. A drive down Purcells Cove Road through the forest of trees crystallized by an ice storm. Sun lighting up the book storage basement of Fernwood Publishing where I'm sending comp copies to university teachers across the country. (There's often sun, somehow—are older memories primarily memories of light?) First burlesque show with a live band. First drag king show. Sunday evening in downtown Halifax and not a soul on the streets when I needed to ask somebody directions. Bob & Lori's food emporium on Gottingen Street and its bright walls and salmon cakes. The attic room above where I paced and danced while listening to Gilles Vigneault and Jacques Brel on the CD walkman. Long, bright day of Halifax rain on my thirtieth birthday. (Five years after I moved out of that building and Halifax altogether, an infant girl dies in those rooms above Bob & Lori's. Dies on the watch of her immigrant student parents from Bangladesh. Her father is later convicted of assault and manslaughter.) A food court in Dartmouth, a counter, its deep fryer and flat grill. Owner of the food establishment who peed in the sink when sure nobody was watching. An almost-fire in the rooming house on South Street that made us all spend the night outside (me, in the computer science building on Dalhousie campus which is alive at all hours and has comfy couches in secluded corners). Hours and hours on the conversation forum Babble on Rabble dot ca, where multiple intense and political online friendships were formed with people from around the country. (None were to survive in real life.) Date with my fencing instructor at a proper restaurant, who later told me she's not gay (the rainbow flags on her fencing gear bags nevertheless). Disabled immigration officer with a walking stick who had bad news for me. A physician who performed the general health check-up for my permanent residence application who kindly suggested I re-do some test, as the bureaucrats might decide to be difficult about a slightly increased white blood cell count. A night at a pub with some colleagues where at one point all the male voices abandoned their respective conversations to join in the singing of Stan Rogers's "Barrett's Privateers" and moreover knew every word (WTF is happening with meter in that song?). An exciting day volunteering all alone in my MP's office on election day, taking phone calls from citizens who don't know what polling station to go to and finding their match through the postal code lookup, then locking up and heading to the school gym nearby to volunteer as a scrutineer at a polling station. Renting the mortarboard and robe for the graduation ceremony. Falling for my tango instructor, what a cliché (when the entire business model for dance instructors is people falling for them) and her letting me know eventually that my attention and emails, which she shared with her partner, reenergized her relationship. First visit to Montreal, listening to Diane Dufresne while exploring the streets. Two reconstructed childhood rooms in Louise Bourgeois exhibition in the Museum of Contemporary Art. Dinner at Délice du Roy in Quebec City. Standing on the Alexandra Bridge in Ottawa, looking at Parliament Hill, awed by the views (and later learning how grim Ottawa is when you move away from the water). First Question Period from the gallery of the House of Commons, a lunch in the Centre Block cafeteria with my MP, Alexa McDonough. At Dalhousie, a feminist philosophy professor talking for almost an hour about the importance of Heidegger for environmental activism, while holding her toddler son (babysitter cancelled on short notice). Toni Morrison stopping by to give a public lecture in a large hall, saying jazz is for everyone, jazz, while of specific cultural origin, is universal, anybody can partake. Having coffee with a Buddhist Haligonian; we don't really have a doctrine, we don't believe in a God, he's telling me; all kinds of ways of being can be Buddhist. (Halifax turns out to be a Buddhist centre of sorts, thanks to the Shambhala Centre.) Final week in Halifax before moving to Toronto, dancing to the electronic tango band Gotan Project, following my pony-tailed Filipino dance partner's wide circles around the empty dance space. (He will inherit my VHS player. The rest of the furniture will be given away on Freecycle.)

First Toronto home, a room in a house on Ossington Avenue, north of Hallam Street, in Bloordale, the land of the Portuguese nata. The roaring Ossington bus. Long trips to a vocational college at the edge of town. Miked teaching to power-point, a course on everything. Reading

Chekhov's *Uncle Vanya* out loud with a class of adult learners in a boardroom in Mississauga. First Toronto Pride. A UCC church with a female minister who had a DDiv in queer theology (the term queer still had a meaning for me then, or so I thought). Church community events, raffle nights, book clubs and my last effort to reconsider Christianity, this time Protestantism, before the endeavour is completely abandoned. Office job in a tower on Don Mills Road in which all the daily tasks are done in the first two to four hours and the rest of the day one needs to sit at the desk, browse databases and pretend to work. (Turns out all the subsequent office jobs will come with that same feature: empty time.) Bar Chicago on Queen West (closed for good since), where a married woman I fancied kissed me; Gatto Nero on College (also closed), where she told me she regrets it and that we are stopping. A different office job: first in a series that were primarily affective labour, the main component of administrative and assistantship jobs. First visit to the Canadian Opera Company, fifth tier tickets for Prokofiev's *War and Peace*. A pass to the Hot Docs Festival the year I discover the thrill of free speech in a shared space during the Q&A after a Danish documentary about the Mohammed cartoons, and an Israeli one which asks if the Anti-Defamation League is inflating accusations of anti-Semitism (either film would have come with social media de-platforming campaigns in the year 2022, if they'd even made the festival programming). Pausing on the Baldwin Steps on Spadina, turning to look south. After first full day of bicycling, I dream of riding, the scenery passing before my REM eyes, wind blowing. Spadina House staffer rhapsodizing about wall paper. At a particularly bleak, fair to say depressing time, finding myself in Montgomery's Inn during an early music festival, and walking to a room where the consort of five viols are talking technique, strategizing among friends, then playing, and the lighting in the room completely changes, the sun comes in. Citizenship ceremony on St Clair East. The musky wet smell of the ravines in summer. Carefree, youthful liveliness of Hart House, somebody playing the piano, a wedding party at the quadrant posing for the official photographer. Respectably attended first book launch in the Drake Hotel (fast forward to the second one, in a favourite Dundas St café on a hot July, where only nine people show). First good reviews, first mixed reviews. *Her flashes of brilliance do not make up for her literary lapses.* At a wine bar in Distillery District interviewing a visual arts donor about his reasons for donating; "Vancouver school of photography is one of the great things this country has produced", the old man of the Rogers family says. A job interview at the home of a former governor general who upon reading where I'm from asks me if I've seen the very risqué Dusan Makavejev-directed Swedish-co production movie *Montenegro*. (I hadn't! I've since learned it has nothing to do with the actual Montenegro.) The discovery of yoga, which taps into reservoirs of sadness I did not know I had, and dissolves them. Hearing for the first time the recognizable South Slav vowels in an early performance of Ana Sokolović's a cappella opera *Svadba*, which will become the most frequently performed Canadian opera of the following decade. The final scene of Robert Lepage's *Lipsynch* in which, in a reversed Pietà, a female body is held by a male. Atom Egoyan's version of the myth of Hercules, *Cruel & Tender*. (Classical music lovers running into Atom Egoyan in concert halls.) An online dating app that offers a lot of sapiosexuals, heteroflexibles and the astrology-obsessed in the women-for-women section. *Look, I'm kind of straight.* And *I live in Chicago, can't really share my real name.* And *I'd never date an Aries.* A repurposed flower shop in the Junction turned into a studio apartment: a home for ten years. A *Tristan und Isolde* performance from the orchestra pit, seated next to the second violins, violas and cellos, the score on lap: thunder and honey. Labyrinthine back offices of the Canadian Opera Company where I'm meeting David

McVicar for an interview. Cafés, so many cafés. The ten marvellous minutes that I was the *Globe and Mail*'s opera critic. The fairy tale that is Edwards Gardens in late summer. Making people laugh at a book event in London, Ont; throwing a decent book shindig with four other writers in Hamilton (the café has since, surprise, closed for good). Wild swimming in the Niagara river, some kilometres away by bicycle from the Falls: Iris Murdoch would have approved. All the flat tires in Toronto, all the potholes, and those few surprisingly smooth roads. Junkies shooting up in the open in Moss Park, other junkies firing up the crack pipe on the stairs to the Rosedale ravine. Wind howling through construction sites. All the snack stands at City of Toronto-owned skating rinks, which somehow move me, perhaps it's the dash of socialist Yugoslavia, or a dash of a *Gemeinschaft*? The institution that is the Zamboni. Koi fish pool in a front yard garden in Cabbagetown. So much personality in the faces in the first room of the National Gallery of Canada, the earliest Canadian portraiture, the Quebecois bourgeois looking back at the viewer with a twinkle in the eye. Talking to the composer André Ristic at the interval in the plush Koerner Hall in my mother tongue (the Quebecois composer picked it up from his father's side of the family and he travels to Montenegro more often than I do). Masks of the North West at the National Gallery of Canada, which are, Claude Levi Strauss argued ardently, at the same level of artistic achievement as the ancient Egyptian or European medieval art. Any painting by Clarence Gagnon that makes it into my Twitter timeline. Earnest urban affairs nerdiness of the group of people that founded the *Spacing* magazine that came out during the David Miller's mayoralty. Next mayor, Rob Ford, caught on video speaking a monologue in Jamaican patois in a late-night take-out spot. The current mayor, expressing his displeasure that a feminist was able to book a room for a talk at the Toronto Public Library—news I read, upset and disappointed, on my phone while on a street in Paris, waiting for the long-planned sibling reunion to start, my mind far away from the upstanding TPL, and Mayor Tory's illiberal stance. The slow swish of the kayak paddle against water around the Toronto Centre Island. A similarly calming swish, different lighting, season, and paddle (canoe), on a lake in Ottawa off the Rideau Canal. Coming across John A. Macdonald's house in Kingston. Pots of tea at a mid-town Italian restaurant in Toronto where the writing of this book was discussed for the first time. Bird song on the tree crowns of Earl Street sometimes beginning as early as 3:30 a.m. in the summer. All the creeks of Toronto. All the stubbornly *closed for the winter* toilets in parks. All the bike mechanics who've tuned and replaced and pumped air and talked too fast. One particularly favourite IPA by a microbrewer in the Junction. Salmon jumping the barriers upstream on the Humber River in October, eager to home and mate, capped by a certain death. All the red-winged black birds attacking passers-by in Toronto's parks in the spring. Learning to skate in my forties. The new streetcars, which are less pleasant to be in than the old streetcars. The Did You Know? tab on the Environment Canada weather app which demystifies wind. All the unruly polar bears which will spend the night in jail cells in Churchill, Manitoba. All the deer and white mountain peaks and chocolate fudge from the main drag in Banff, Alberta. The wind howling outside my fifteenth-floor windows. The lucky fact that the rain never stays for too long.

This life. This country. To be continued?

Acknowledgements

THANK YOU Ken Whyte for understanding my writing exactly as I hoped it would be understood. I'm lucky to have found Sutherland House. Shalomi Ranasinghe, Matthew Bucemi, Serina Mercier, Sarah Miniaci: I owe you all drinks. My thanks also go to Jennifer Westaway whose proofreading and fact-checking acumen saved me from myself at several junctures in the manuscript.

I am grateful to Lari Langford of the University of Toronto Library for letting me purchase the Research Reader membership at the time of the bleakest winter lockdown, when the U of T Library looked like it was not at all sure if it wanted to open its book vaults to external researchers for a good while yet. Those four months of access to curbside pickups were a lifeline.

Many thanks to Božena Jelušić and Snježana Milivojević for sharing their knowledge with me. Hearing Božena Jelušić speak about Mihailo Lalić in an interview that I came across on YouTube is what set me on the path of reconnecting with Montenegrin culture.

This book is for my sisters, Nevenka Vukmirović and Nataša Perović-Mikulas.

Notes

CHAPTER 1

The epigraph is from Alice Munro, *Selected Stories* (Toronto: Penguin Canada, 1998)

The verse in the first sentence is of course from Dante's *Inferno*, which has been read over the last century as (also) a book about mid-life crisis, and perhaps what we would today call depression. There are numerous translations in verse and in prose, and there's also a video game. Robert Pinsky's 1996 translation is a good in; former *Guardian* book critic Nicholas Lezard found Ciaran Carson's 'most readable'.

". . . at least until Paul Martin and Mike Harris." Both Martin's 1993 budget, which stopped federal spending on affordable housing, and the 'deficit-slaying' 1995 budget, which severely cut programs, radically changed Canada, until then on a fairly Scandinavian-ish path. "It cut government spending, not just in real terms, after inflation is accounted for, which is rare enough, but also in nominal terms, something that had not been seen since before the Second World War, and it did so for two years running. It remade federal-provincial fiscal relations by completing the switch from tied to block grants initiated in 1977 by the Trudeau government. It did away with the Crow Rate rail transportation subsidies that had stood since 1897. It cut the CBC to such an extent the corporation's president resigned in protest the next day. It reduced Unemployment Insurance benefits and it promised, though it did not deliver, a reform of old age security, a decision that caused a last-minute dispute between Martin and Chrétien." William Watson, 'The Budget That Changed Canada', Fraser Institute 2020, https://financialpost.com/opinion/william-watson-the-budget-that-changed-canada

"Canadian governments implemented much deeper reductions in government program spending than any other major industrialized country – including those (like Italy) which faced even more severe fiscal problems. General government program spending measured as a share of GDP, declined by 10 percentage points in Canada between 1992 and 2002. In the OECD as a whole, over the same period, program spending stayed roughly constant as a share of GDP. So while most OECD countries balanced their budgets during the late 1990s, this goal was not attained in other countries by slashing and burning government programs. Indeed, countries like the U.S., Germany, and France restored fiscal balance with hardly any spending cuts at all – and in some cases, while actually increasing government spending." Jim Stanford, "Paul Martin, the Deficit, and the Debt, Alternative Federal Budget Technical Paper #1," Centre for Future Work, Nov 28, 2003, https://centreforfuturework.ca/wp-content/uploads/2021/06/AFB-2004-Tech-Paper-Paul-Martin-Deficit-Debt.pdf

Mike Harris as Premier of Ontario cut programs, infrastructure projects, and income tax in Ontario. https://en.wikipedia.org/wiki/Mike_Harris#Common_Sense_Revolution While the federal government downloaded the cost of running programs to the provinces, some provinces downloaded those to the cities. The uploading back has not taken place to any significant degree.

Urban planner Gil Meslin tracks the Toronto Open Data updates on Toronto Community Housing, and the chart on building new affordable housing has largely stayed flat. https://twitter.com/g_meslin/status/1219773654529007616 Co-ops have not been built since the 1990s either, though the city of Toronto does introduce the odd small project here and there, like the mid-income building project Housing Now, recently initiated.

Ernest Renan's 1882 lecture *Qu'est-ce qu'une nation?* is available online http:// ucparis.fr/files/9313/6549/9943/What_is_a_Nation.pdf and in many anthologies on nations and nationalism. He foresaw, against the grain of the era and his own continent, that the nation is something that can't be built on 'race', origins, religion or even language, but that it is a daily referendum, an expression of solidarity across time and place, a narration, and a strategic forgetting as much as remembering.

"Only connect" is of course from E.M. Forster's novel *Howards End*, forgive if I state the obvious. "Only connect the prose and the passion, and both will be exalted, and human love will be seen at its height. Live in fragments no longer. Only connect, and the beast and the monk, robbed of the isolation that is life to either, will die." With Doris Lessing's *The Golden Notebook* some decades later, the problem of disconnect, compartmentalization and "code switching" raises its head again.

Quand on n'est nulle part, on pense; quand on n'est nulle part, on écrit. Julia Kristeva said this in a French TV interview that I watched many years ago and, in different ways, in her writings about being a stranger, both in a new country and a stranger to one self, psychoanalytically. Main source is Julia Kristeva, *Strangers to Ourselves*, trans. Leon S. Roudiez, (New York: Columbia University Press, 1991), and the many books it inspired, for example, *The Kristeva Critical Reader*, John Lechte and Mary Zournazi eds., (Edinburgh: Edinburgh University Press, 2003), especially the pieces by Ewa Ziarek and Miglena Nikolchina, and *Foreign Dialogues*, ed. Mary Zournazi (London: Pluto Press 1998). The melancholic is "a stranger in his mother tongue", writes Kristeva in *Black Sun: Depression and Melancholia* (New York: Columbia University Press, 1992).

CHAPTER 2

I first learned about the Huron ossuary in Adam Bunch's *The Toronto Book of the Dead* (Toronto: Dundurn Press, 2017). It's an undervisited, off the radar place. The Historicist, which was a regular feature of the now defunct publication *Torontoist*, tells a detailed story of the discovery and contextualization at https://torontoist.com/2015/02/historicist-the-tabor-hill-ossuary/.

The North American branch of The Seven Years' War, probably the first global war in history, transformed Canada and added it to the British empire. There are useful pages about it and the indigenous participation on the Britannica online, and I'd recommend the episode about the Seven Years' War on the podcast *The Rest is History* hosted by Dominic Sandbrook and Tom Holland with the British TV celeb historian guest Dan Snow a.k.a. Margaret MacMillan's nephew. The Crash Course video that can be found on YouTube on what the Americans called the French and Indian War is, in spite a couple of silly turns, also useful.

Gary Mason, "The Wet'suwet'en deal could be a recipe for disaster," *The Globe and Mail*, May 26, 2020. John Ivison, "Trudeau's failure to reform First Nations politics is the root cause of #shutdowncanada," *The National Post*, February 14, 2020. Chris Selley, "Canada on the brink of terminal gridlock," *The National Post*, February 14, 2020.

Paul Basken, "Carleton University moves to mandate Indigenous teaching: National move to reconciliation tests boundaries of academic freedom, say some observers," Times Higher Education, May 23, 2020, https://www.timeshighereducation.com/news/carleton-university-moves-mandate-indigenous-teaching

Bonnie Allen, Alicia Bridges, "Case of killer's poetry ignites conversation about Indigenization and academic freedom: 'Sometimes you have to just pick one over the other,' says Indigenous student centre manager" CBC News January 4, 2020, https://www.cbc.ca/news/canada/saskatchewan/indigenization-academic-freedom-george-elliott-clarke-steven-kummerfield-1.5414821

The Society for Academic Freedom and Scholarship's archives page is helpful for anyone interested in how job ads for academic positions in Canada have changed.

It's acceptable and even desirable to require exclusively candidates of a specific ethnicity in job postings. https://safs.ca/case-archives/

Eranthi Swaminathan, "3 Concordia researchers collaborate to engage Indigenous knowledges in the study of physics: A New Frontiers in Research Fund grant will support interdisciplinary approaches to decolonizing science," Concordia September 20, 2019, https://www.concordia.ca/news/stories/2019/09/20/3-concordia-researchers-collaborate-to-engage-indigenous-knowledges-in-the-study-of-physics.html

Poppy Noor, "A playwright wants only critics of color to review her. Here's what our own critics think," *The Guardian* February 21, 2020, https://www.theguardian.com/culture/2020/feb/21/yolanda-bonnell-playwright-criticism-color

Karen Fricker, Carly Maga, "Jesse Wente's goal as new Chair of the Canada Council for the Arts? To reduce the harm it causes," *The Toronto Star* August 6, 2020, https://www.thestar.com/entertainment/2020/08/06/jesse-wentes-goal-as-new-chair-of-the-canada-council-for-the-arts-to-reduce-the-harm-it-causes.html

Jon Kay, "'Canada Has Gone Mad': Indigenous Representation and the Hounding of Angie Abdou," *Quillette* January 10, 2018, https://quillette.com/2018/01/10/canada-gone-mad-indigenous-representation-hounding-angie-abdou/

"Modern Treaties," the Crown-Indigenous Relations and Northern Affairs Canada website, under Treaties, Agreements and Negotiations, accessed November 6, 2021, https://www.rcaanc-cirnac.gc.ca/eng/1100100028574/1529354437231#chp4

Brian Giesbrecht, "Who Pressured Whom?" *C2C Journal* March 11, 2019, https://c2cjournal.ca/2019/03/who-pressured-whom/

"Murdered and Missing Indigenous Women and Girls," Canadian Femicide Observatory for Justice and Accountability, accessed November 6, 2021, http://www.femicideincanada.ca/about/history/indigenous

"Suicide among First Nations people, Métis and Inuit (2011-2016): Findings from the 2011 Canadian Census Health and Environment Cohort (CanCHEC),"

Statistics Canada, accessed November 6, 2021, www150.statcan.gc.ca "Statistical Overview on the Overrepresentation of Indigenous Persons in the Canadian Correctional System and Legislative Reforms to Address the Problem," Government of Canada Department of Justice, accessed November 6, 2021 https://www.justice.gc.ca/eng/rp-pr/jr/gladue/p2.html

Kazi Stastna, "Shacks and slop pails: infrastructure crisis on native reserves. Spending on housing and water in First Nations communities not keeping up with need" CBC News November 26, 2011, https://www.cbc.ca/news/canada/shacks-and-slop-pails-infrastructure-crisis-on-native-reserves-1.1004957

'I might have been indigenous to the land itself, but I was a first-generation cultural immigrant to the United States', from Kate Tuttle's article, "Sherman Alexie on his new memoir, his mother and Donald Trump," *The Los Angeles Times* July 7, 2017, https://www.latimes.com/books/jacketcopy/la-ca-jc-sherman-alexie-20170707-story.html

Alex Bozikovic, Cheryll Case, John Lorinc, Annabel Vaughan, eds., *House Divided: How the Missing Middle Will Solve Toronto's Affordability Crisis* (Toronto: Coach House Books, 2019).

CHAPTER 3

David Gorski, "An aboriginal girl dies of leukemia: Parental 'rights' versus the rights of a child to medical care" Science-Based Medicine January 25, 2015, https://sciencebasedmedicine.org/a-tale-of-two-children-dying-from-cancer-one-past-one-future/. Bill Graveland, The Canadian Press, "We can move on with our lives': Alberta parents acquitted in death of toddler" CTVNews.ca December 19, 2019, https://www.ctvnews.ca/canada/we-can-move-on-with-our-lives-alberta-parents-acquitted-in-death-of-toddler-1.4600881

Rosie DiManno, "Whose courts best serve Indigenous women and children?," *The Toronto Star* September 11, 2018, https://www.thestar.com/opinion/star-columnists/2018/09/11/whose-courts-best-serve-indigenous-women-and-children.html

Catharine Tunney, "Trudeau says deaths and disappearances of Indigenous women and girls amount to 'genocide,'" CBC News June 4, 2019, https://www.cbc.ca/news/politics/trudeau-mmiwg-genocide-1.5161681

We read in class, by Charles Taylor et al, *Multiculturalism: Examining the Politics of Recognition*, ed. Amy Gutmann (Princeton: Princeton University Press, 1994). Also, Andrew Kernohan, *Liberalism, Equality, and Cultural Oppression* (Cambridge: Cambridge University Press, 1998).

James Tully, "On Global Citizenship," in *On Global Citizenship: James Tully in Dialogue* (London: Bloomsbury, 2014), 7, 19 and later ibid, 31.

Zack Beauchamp, "The amazing decline of global hunger, in one chart," Vox October 13, 2014, https://www.vox.com/2014/10/13/6969953/malnutrition-undernutrition-getting-better World Health Organization, "Children: Improving Survival and Well-Being," WHO International September 8, 2020. A good listen on this topic is the May 25, 2021 episode of radio station KERA's *Think* podcast, hosted by Krys Boyd, with guest Steven Johnson. He talks about his book *Extra Life: A Short History of Living Longer* (New York: Riverhead Books, 2021), and how humans managed to double their life expectancy over the last century.

From OurWorldInData.org: "Since the beginning of the age of the Enlightenment the mortality of children has declined rapidly. Child mortality in rich countries today is much lower than 1%. This is a very recent development and was only reached after a hundredfold decline in child mortality in these countries. In early-modern times, child mortality was very high; in 18th century Sweden every third child died, and in 19th century Germany every second child died. With declining poverty and increasing knowledge and service in the health sector, child mortality around the world is declining very rapidly: Global child mortality fell from 19% in 1960 to just below 4% in 2017; while 4% is still too high, this is a substantial achievement." https://ourworldindata.org/child-mortality#child-mortality-around-the-world-since-1800

There are some heated conversations around the so-called de-growth movement, which argues that the planet can't tolerate economic growth at this pace. However, economic prosperity usually coincides with a decrease in infant mortality, so some critics have used this correlation to slam the de-growthers for not having worked out all the consequences. Tom Chivers did a persuasive dunk on the de-growthers in "Who would kill children to save the planet?," Unherd August 13, 2021. One of the key de-growth thinkers, Jason Hickel, replied (in a link-filled Twitter thread: https://mobile.twitter.com/jasonhickel/status/1426177142849773570) that Chivers used a strawman argument and misquoted their ideas. De-growth, he says, explicitly focuses on wealthy countries, not countries in development, and to miss that is to miss a major point.

Alex Bozikovic, "After COVID-19, city parks need to make room for everyone," *The Globe and Mail*, July 31, 2020, https://www.theglobeandmail.com/canada/toronto/article-after-covid-19-city-parks-need-to-make-room-for-everyone/

Robin Cook, "Only we and Lesotho reserve seats for hereditary chieftains," *The Guardian*, February 18, 2005, https://www.theguardian.com/politics/2005/feb/18/lords.constitution On the government of Canada's website, the page titled 'Child, early and forced marriage' states: "Each year, an estimated 12 million girls aged under 18 marry against their will." https://www.international.gc.ca/world-monde/issues_development-enjeux_developpement/human_rights-droits_homme/child_marriage-mariages_enfants.aspx?lang=eng

Predrag Tomović, "Nestaje običaj muškog nasljeđivanja u Crnoj Gori", Radio Free Europe, April 3, 2019. https://www.slobodnaevropa.org/a/pravo-na-imovinu-rod-%C5%BEene-dom/29859105.html

James Tully, *Strange Multiplicity: Constitutionalism in an Age of Diversity* (Cambridge: Cambridge University Press, 1995), p. 63 and 183-4, 172.

For more on Thomas Hobbes, key theorist of state sovereignty as we understand it today, it's worth listening to the 2020 History of Ideas series from the podcast *Talking* Politics. (The episode on Thomas Hobbes's *Leviathan* delivered by David Runciman is at https://www.talkingpoliticspodcast.com/history-of-ideas-1) Even better, the *Shakespeare & Company* podcast episode where Adam Biles talks to David Runciman about his book, *Confronting Leviathan*, (London: Profile Books, 2021).

Says Runciman: "What the book is saying is not how bad life can be, but how good life can be. In the seventeenth century here's someone writing and saying, if we get this right, if we can anchor our politics in a way that gives people the security they need, so they're not constantly fighting each other, the advantage would be not just wealth (we'll become rich), not just peace (we'll live longer), not just contentment, but it will free us from politics. The trouble with the world he lived in was that politics was everywhere. You couldn't go to sleep at night confident that you'd wake up the next morning and politics wouldn't have invaded your home and taken away your children. Wouldn't it be wonderful to live in a world where politics was just a kind of background fact. That's his dream. And we live in a world where . . . actually one of the things that we've discovered in the last few years is just how miserable it can make us when politics comes back. One of the things that modern citizens have become slightly addicted to is the luxury of not having to worry about politics."

Janet Ajzenstat, *The Once and Future Canadian Democracy* (Montreal: McGill-Queen's University Press, 2003).

Kenneth McNaught, *Conscience and History: A Memoir* (Toronto: University of Toronto Press, 1999).

Dominic Sandbrook's review of the book *Black Spartacus: The Epic Life of Toussaint Louverture* by Sudhir Hazareesingh, ran in *The Sunday Times*, November 22, 2020. Mary Wollstonecraft's 1792 *A Vindication of the Rights of Women* is available in its entirety on Bartleby.com. Immanuel Kant's 1784 essay "Answering the Question: What is Enlightenment?" is also easily found online in different translations. It, and another of Kant's key political texts on liberalism, "Perpetual Peace: A Philosophical Sketch," with some other essays, are assembled in *Kant: Political Writings*, ed. H.S. Reiss, (Cambridge: Cambridge University Press, [1970] 1991). Some of Kant's other occasional pieces have aged less well.

Alasdair MacIntyre, in *After Virtue* (Notre Dame: University of Notre Dame Press, 1981) declares Mozart and Kant the two key figures of the Continental Enlightenment and I've always found that neat and persuasive. For Mozart at his most sunny, internationalist and pro-worker, see *The Marriage of Figaro* (libretto by

Lorenzo da Ponte, based on Beaumarchais's play), *The Abduction from the Seraglio* (Emanuel Schikaneder) and, up to a point, *The Magic Flute* (Schikaneder). *Don Giovanni* is altogether darker and borderline Romantic; *The Clemency of Titus* is a quaint paean to the wisdom of an enlightened absolutist – granted, containing some killer mezzosoprano-in-trousers arias; with *Così fan tutte*, Da Ponte messed up Marivaux's 1744 play *La Dispute* and created the only Mozart opera that feels endless. Don't @ me.

Richard Rorty, *Philosophy and Social Hope* (London: Penguin, 1999).

The Biographi.ca page on Robert Baldwin is very useful. Michael S. Cross and Robert Lochiel Fraser, "BALDWIN, ROBERT," in *Dictionary of Canadian Biography*, vol. 8, University of Toronto/Université Laval, 2003–, accessed November 27, 2021, http://www.biographi.ca/en/bio/baldwin_robert_8E.html

CabbageTownPeople.ca has a quick intro to Baldwin, and the TorontoHistory.net article "Spadina I and Spadina II" gives a backgrounder on the Baldwin family's stomping grounds, Spadina House. The property, later acquired by the Austins, now houses a museum.

Karl Popper, *The Open Society and Its Enemies* (Abingdon: Routledge, 1945). Richard Rorty, *Contingency, Irony, Solidarity* (Cambridge: Cambridge University Press, 1989).

CHAPTER 4

There is an extensive argument among several writers about *The Second Sex* translations in English on the *London Review of Books* website, starting with the print issue Vol. 32 No. 3, 11 February 2010 and the piece "The Adulteress Wife" by Toril Moi (https://www.lrb.co.uk/the-paper/v32/n03/toril-moi/the-adulteress-wife). The long awaited second translation—which was to improve on the first and abridged by H. M. Parshley—apparently comes with its own plethora of not negligible flaws. I, however, have consulted this newer translation, as it's the only complete one: Simone de Beauvoir, *The Second Sex*, trans. Constance Borde and Sheila Malovany-Chevallier, (New York: Vintage Books, 2011). Especially the chapters "The Married Woman" and "The Mother" in the second volume are of use here. There's been a lot of new de Beauvoir scholarship lately, and I've enjoyed Manon Garcia's *We Are Not Born Submissive: How Patriarchy Shapes Women's Lives* (Princeton: Princeton University Press, 2021), as well as Meryl Altman's *Beauvoir in Time* (Leiden: Brill | Rodopi Press, 2020). The first two sections of Altman, "Unhappy Bodies" and "Lesbian Lived Experience", are particularly pertinent. Kate Fitzpatrick's bio *Becoming Beauvoir: A Life* (London: Bloomsbury Academic, 2019) does a good job of disentangling Beauvoir's philosophy from Sartre's. Sarah Bakewell's *At the Existentialist Café: Freedom, Being, and Apricot Cocktails* (Toronto: Knopf Canada, 2016) is just excellent overall on the existentialists of all kinds.

Doris Lessing, *The Golden Notebook* (New York: Harper Perennial Modern Classics, [1962] 2008).

What an extraordinary book D. W. Winnicott's *The Child, the Family and the Outside World* is! (Cambridge: Perseus Publishing, [1957, 1964] 1987). Alison Bechdel's graphic memoir *Are You My Mother* (Boston: Houghton Mifflin, 2012) is a fine appreciation of this lesser read psychoanalyst.

Chantal Akerman, *My Mother Laughs*, trans. Corina Copp, (New York: The Song Cave (2019).

The man who wrote interesting things about the homosociality of friendship and its inability – in philosophy – to incorporate sexual difference was Jacques Derrida, *The Politics of Friendship*, trans. George Collins, (London: Verso, 2006). Richard Rorty hit the nail on the head about Derrida: "I agree with Drucilla Cornell that one of Derrida's central contributions to feminism is that 'he explicitly argues that fundamental philosophical questions cannot be separated from the thinking of sexual difference' (Cornell, 1991, 98). Indeed, I should go further and say that Derrida's most original and important contribution to philosophy is his weaving together of Freud and Heidegger, his association of 'ontological difference' with gender difference. This weaving together enables us to see for the first time the connection between the philosophers' quest for purity, the view that women are somehow impure, the subordination of women, and 'virile homosexuality' (the kind of male homosexuality that Eve Sedgwick calls 'homo-homosexuality', epitomized in Jean Genet's claim that 'the man who fucks another man is twice a man'). Compared to this insight (which is most convincingly put forward in Derrida's *Geschlecht I*), the grab bag of easily reproduced gimmicks labelled 'deconstruction' seems to me relatively unimportant." Rorty, "Feminism, Ideology, and Deconstruction: A Pragmatist View," *Hypatia* 8, no. 2 (Spring 1993): 102-3.

Just some of the writers of the poetics of female friendship: Elena Ferrante, Margaret Drabble, Margarethe von Trotta, Zadie Smith, Victoria Wood, Céline Sciamma, Sheila Heti. But not Atwood, whose *Cat's Eye* is clear-eyed (heh) on how evil girls and women can be to one another.

Ray Pahl, "Towards a more significant sociology of friendship," *European Journal of Sociology / Archives Européennes de Sociologie* 43, no. 3 (2002): 410-423. For further pointers, see this from William McBride, *Philosophical Reflections on the Changes in Eastern Europe* (Lanham: Rowman and Littlefield, 1999), "It may be objected that these cultural elites are part of the social froth of society and are not involved in the engine room of change. There is much evidence from Eastern Europe before the so-called velvet revolutions of 1989 that this certainly need not be so. Apart from the detailed autobiographical account by Vaclav Havel and others, there is a brilliant sociological account by Konrad and Szelenyi (Konrad, G. and Szelenyi, I., *The Intellectuals on the Road to Class Power*, New York, Harcourt, Brace, Jovanovich, 1979), which situates the Intelligentsia in a broad sociological canvass."

Alice Echols, *Daring to Be Bad: Radical Feminism in America 1967-1975*, 30th anniversary ed. (Minnesota: University of Minnesota Press, 2019). Rachel Blau DuPlessis and Ann Snitow, eds., *The Feminist Memoir Project* (New Brunswick: Rutgers University Press, 2007).

Noreena Hertz: *The Lonely Century: How to Restore Human Connection in a World That's Pulling Apart* (New York: Currency, 2021), 6: "In Germany two-thirds of the population believed loneliness to be a serious problem. Almost a third of Dutch nationals admitted to being lonely, one in ten severely so. In Sweden, up to a quarter of the population said they were frequently lonely. In Switzerland two out of every five people reported sometimes, often, or always feeling so. In the UK, the problem had become so significant that in 2018 the prime minister went so far as to appoint a Minister for Loneliness. [. . .] Three-quarters of citizens did not know their neighbours' names, whilst 60% of UK employees reported feeling lonely at work."

There's growing research on loneliness, some of it quite bleak. See the report "Age of Alienation: The collapse in community and belonging among young people, and how we should respond," UKonward, July 2021, https://www. ukonward.com/reports/age-of-alienation-loneliness-young-people/ See also Rachel Carlyle, "Men and loneliness: The friendship recession," *The Times* (London), July 17, 2021. Aside from policy think tanks and the media, sociologists too are increasingly interested in friendship and under what conditions it thrives.

Alissa Quart in *Squeezed: Why Our Families Can't Afford America* (New York: Ecco, 2018), documents why becoming and staying middle class has been getting harder and harder in the US. Larry Getlen, "America's middle class is slowly being 'wiped out'," MarketWatch, July 23, 2018, https://www.marketwatch.com/story/ americas-middle-class-is-slowly-being-wiped-out-2018-07-23 Thomas Piketty's *Capital in the Twenty-First Century* looks at the same phenomenon, more widely and longitudinally: the wealth from capital has been dwarfing the income earnings, and the trend will continue. Matthew Yglesias' intro to Piketty's doorstopper is useful: "The short guide to Capital in the 21st Century," Vox, April 8, 2014, https://www.vox.com/2014/4/8/5592198/the-short-guide-to-capital-in-the-21st-century The Peterson Institute for International Economics microsite "How to Fix Economic Inequality? An Overview of Policies for the United States and Other High-Income Economies" has the details on how "[i]ncome inequality has grown within advanced economies as top earners have experienced more rapid income growth and bottom earners were left behind." https://www.piie.com/ microsites/how-fix-economic-inequality

Regarding "neoliberalism". Everybody and their cat has been using the word to mean "whatever I don't like about the economy/society of the last four decades" but I would like to insist that neoliberalism is still a useful term delineating an actual phenomenon. The clearest and most historically informed thing I've read about neoliberalism recently was a piece by James Meadway, "Neoliberalism is dying—now we must replace it," OpenDemocracy.net, September 3, 2021, https://beta.opendemocracy.net/en/oureconomy/neoliberalism-is-dying-now-we-must-replace-it/

For Toronto and developers, see the earlier quoted *The House Divided* (Bozikovic et al. eds.). Bruce Campion Smith, "More Toronto residents in apartments than detached houses, census finds," *The Toronto Star*, May 3, 2017, https://www.thestar.com/news/canada/2017/05/03/more-toronto-residents-in-apartments-than-detached-houses-census-finds.html Also, "Toronto Housing Market Analysis: From Insight to Action, a report by Canadian Centre for Economic Analysis and Canadian Urban Institute," January 2019, https://www.toronto.ca/legdocs/mmis/2019/ph/bgrd/backgroundfile-124480.pdf And "The GTA Rental Market is Starting to Resemble its Pre-COVID Level," Storeys, July 19, 2021, https://storeys.com/toronto-leading-gta-rental-market-recovery-q2/

Naomi Powell, "Want to buy a Toronto condo? You now need an annual income of at least $100,000," *Financial Post*, April 11, 2018, https://financialpost.com/real-estate/want-to-buy-a-toronto-condo-you-now-need-an-annual-income-of-at-least-100000 The disappearing Georgian façades can be found in *Old Toronto Houses* by Tom Cruickshank and John de Visser, (Richmond Hill: Firefly Books, 2008).

Aleksandar Hemon, *The Book of My Lives* (New York: Farrar, Straus & Giroux, 2013).

Sarah Gomillion, "Peak friendship: data reveals when you'll be most popular," TheConversation, April 6, 2016, https://theconversation.com/peak-friendship-data-reveals-when-youll-be-most-popular-57293

Cornelia Wrzus, Martha Hänel, Jenny Wagner, and Franz J. Neyer, "Social network changes and life events across the life span: A meta-analysis," *Psychological Bulletin, 139*(1) (2013): 53–80. "Cross-sectional as well as longitudinal studies consistently showed that (a) the global social network increased up until young adulthood and then decreased steadily, (b) both the personal network and the friendship network decreased throughout adulthood, (c) the family network was stable in size from adolescence to old age, and (d) other networks with coworkers or neighbors were important only in specific age ranges."

"Stig Abell on . . . friendship," *The Sunday Times*, May 17, 2020, https://www.thetimes.co.uk/article/stig-abell-on-friendship-fdwfrm2x9 Claire Bushey, "Loneliness and me," *Financial Times*, November 21, 2020, https://www.ft.com/content/408afd90-7f25-49b9-a10d-253c5b29e743 Josh Glancy, "It's inevitable that friends disappear in your thirties. Life gets in the way," *The Sunday Times*, July 12, 2020, https://www.thetimes.co.uk/article/its-inevitable-that-friends-disappear-in-your-thirties-life-gets-in-the-way-trbpcmhd6

CBC Radio One, "Sunday Edition: '100 years ago, Canada produced beautiful pianos. Now we send them to the dump,'" September 30, 2016.

"85% of us do not feel engaged in our jobs" is from Gallup's State of the Global Workforce Report online https://www.gallup.com/workplace/238079/state-global-workplace-2017.aspx#formheader and cited in Hertz, 2021.

CHAPTER 5

Alexandar Nehamas's *Nietzsche: Life as Literature* (Cambridge: Harvard University Press, 1987), is a delightful intro to Nietzsche, should you ever be in search of one.

Charles Taylor, *The Ethics of Authenticity* (Cambridge: Harvard University Press, [1991] 2018) 40-41.

A newish edition is the Cambridge University Press's 2001 release of Ferdinand Tönnies's *Community and Civil Society*. Max Weber and Emil Durkheim both dialogue with Tönnies's ideas.

Robert D. Putnam, "E Pluribus Unum: Diversity and Community in the Twenty-first Century," The 2006 Johan Skytte Prize Lecture, Wiley Online Library, June 15, 2007, https://onlinelibrary.wiley.com/doi/10.1111/j.1467-9477.2007.00176.x

Christel Kesler and Irene Bloemraad. 2010. "Does Immigration Erode Social Capital? The Conditional Effects of Immigration-Generated Diversity on Trust, Membership and Participation across 19 Countries." Canadian Journal of Political Science/Revue canadienne de science politique, Volume 43, Issue 2: Diversity and Democratic Politics, June 2010.

Dietlind Stolle, Stuart Soroka and Richard Johnston, "When Does Diversity Erode Trust? Neighborhood Diversity, Interpersonal Trust, and the Mediating Effect of Social Interactions." *Political Studies* 56 no.1 (2008) https://onlinelibrary. wiley.com/doi/abs/10.1111/j.1467-9248.2007.00717.x

Christopher J. Anderson and Aida Paskeviciute, "How Ethnic and Linguistic Heterogeneity Influence the Prospects for Civil Society: A Comparative Study of Citizenship Behavior," *The Journal of Politics* 68 no. 4 (2006) https://www. journals.uchicago.edu/doi/10.1111/j.1468-2508.2006.00470.x

Edward Fieldhouse and David Cutts, "Does Diversity Damage Social Capital? A Comparative Study of Neighbourhood Diversity and Social Capital in the US and Britain," *Canadian Journal of Political Science / Revue canadienne de science politique*, 43, no. 2 (June 2010).

Even before Putnam, political sociologists and social psychologists studying trust and distrust found ethnic diversity a factor. "Who trusts others?" by Alberto Alesina and Eliana La Ferrara (*Journal of Public Economics* 85, 2002), "Determinants of generalized trust: A cross-country comparison", the 2007 paper by Christian Bjørnskov (*Public Choice* 130) and research examining potential correlation between diversity and decline of the welfare state, such as the 2002 paper "Ethnicity, Trust, and the Welfare State" by Stuart Neil Soroka, Keith Banting and Richard Johnson published in *Social Capital, Diversity, and the Welfare State*, Fiona Kay and Richard Johnston (eds.), UBC Press, 2006, are among the key contributions on the topic.

Statistics Canada, National Household Survey 2011, Mixed Unions in Canada, archived at https://www12.statcan.gc.ca/nhs-enm/2011/as-sa/99-010-x/99-010-x2011003_3-eng.cfm

Another report is of interest: Statistics Canada, Canadian Social Trends, 11-008-X No. 89 2010001: "A portrait of couples in mixed unions," by Anne Milan, Hélène Maheux and Tina Chui in April 2010. "Since people tend to migrate as adults, they may have already formed unions by the time they immigrate to Canada. Individuals born in Canada, on the other hand, would be more likely to form unions in this country. As such, Canadian-born visible minorities in couples had a higher proportion in mixed unions than their foreign-born counterparts. In 2006, among Canadian-born visible minorities in couples, 56% had a partner or spouse who was either a non-visible minority or was a member of a different visible minority group compared to 12% for those who were foreign-born.

The proportion of visible minorities in couples that were mixed was higher for the Canadian-born compared to the foreign-born for each visible minority group, but there was some variation across groups. More than two-thirds of married or partnered Canadian-born Japanese were in mixed unions (69%), while this was the case for one-half (50%) of all Japanese in couples who were born outside the country. In fact, 48% of Japanese who were born in Japan and were in couples had formed an out-group conjugal union. In contrast, over one-half (54%) of Chinese in couples who were born in Canada were in mixed unions in 2006, whereas this was true for 6% of Chinese born outside the country. Among married or partnered Chinese who were born in China, only 3% were in mixed unions. Similarly, about one-third of Canadian-born South Asians in couples were in mixed unions, while 3% of South Asians born in South Asia were in mixed unions. Among Canadian-born Blacks in couples, 63% were in mixed unions while this was true for 17% of Blacks in couples born in the Caribbean and Bermuda, and 13% of African-born Blacks."

For more Canadian data, the Institute for Research on Public Policy has a substantial section on Diversity, Immigration and Integration which wrapped up in 2015. See also Dietlind Stolle and Allison Harell, "Social Capital and Ethno-racial Diversity: Learning to Trust in an Immigrant Society," *Political Studies* 61 (2013): 42–66. "Using the Canadian General Social Survey (2003), our results show that despite a negative relationship among adults, younger Canadians with racial and ethnic diversity in their social networks show higher levels of generalized trust."

David Bartram, "Happiness and 'economic migration': A comparison of Eastern European migrants and stayers," *Migration Studies* 1 no. 2 (July 2013).

John Gray, "Why this crisis is a turning point in history," *New Statesman*, April 3, 2020. Gray is a sombre reactionary whose brilliant writing seduces you into its world. But one of the best pieces of criticism of Gray's politics that I've read recently is the lucid essay by Jon Bloomfield for OpenDemocracy.org, "John Gray: the nationalist philosopher stoking 'culture wars' fires," October 19, 2020.

Ajzenstat on Taylor in *The Once and Future Canadian Democracy*, p. 122, and that exactly anticipates Taylor's position on Quebec's secularism bill.

Helen Lewis, "The World Is Trapped in America's Culture War: America won the internet, and now makes us all speak its language" *The Atlantic*, October 27, 2020.

CHAPTER 8

For Hodler's Valentine series and other paintings, see Ferdinand Hodler: View to Infinity, the catalogue of a Hodler retrospective held at Neue Galerie, New York, 2012-2013, and at Fondation Beyeler, Basel, 2013.

Paul Benedict Rowan, *Making Ryan's Daughter: The Myths, Madness and Mastery* (Dublin: New Island Books, 2020).

Helen Gardner, ed., *John Donne: The elegies, and the songs and sonnets* (Oxford: Clarendon Press, 1965).

Margaret Edson, *Wit: A Play* (London: Faber & Faber, 1999).

Marina Vujnovic, *Forging the Bubikopf Nation: Journalism, Gender and Modernity in Interwar Yugoslavia* (New York: Peter Lang Publishing, 2009), 45.

Annegret Hoberg, ed., *Alfred Kubin: drawings 1897-1909* (Munich: Prestel, 2008).

Bakewell, *At the Existentialist Café*, 320, 235. For the growing role of algorithms/AI in our lives, see Hannah Fry, *Hello, World: How to Be Human in the Age of the Machine*

(New York: W.W. Norton & Company, 2018). Cees Nooteboom, *The Following Story*, trans. Ina Rilke (New York: Vintage Classics, 2014).

Lee Smolin, *Time Reborn: From the Crisis in Physics to the Future of the Universe* (Boston: Houghton Mifflin Harcourt, 2013) gives one's brain a proper rolfing. What I understood, I loved. It's there that I've learned about Julian Barbour's theories as well.

Jacqueline Rose, *Mothers: An Essay on Love and Cruelty* (New York: Farrar, Straus & Giroux, 2018).

CHAPTER 9

Kevin Richie, "Toronto Public Library facing Pride ban over Meghan Murphy event. Pride's board of directors has released an open letter warning the library that 'there will be consequences to our relationship for this betrayal,'" *NOW*, October 18, 2019. Haley Ryan, "Pride breaks with Halifax libraries after controversial book kept on shelves," CBC News, May 30, 2021. Becky Robertson, "Pride Toronto speaks out against MLSE for hosting Dave Chappelle's sold-out show," BlogTO, November 15, 2021. See also: Kathleen Stock, "Can biological males be lesbians?," The Article, January 14, 2019.

There is a quick but decent intro to the recent history of Montenegro on Princeton University's The Princeton Encyclopedia of Self-Determination website at https://pesd.princeton.edu/node/726 A lot of recent books about the Balkans tend to skim over Montenegro, I presume due to its size or its unfortunate alliance with the expansionist and much bigger Serbia in the 1990s. Montenegro might have been seen then, not entirely unjustifiably, as just a satellite of a major Balkan mover. I managed to find only two books in English published in the last two decades dedicated to Montenegro's history first and foremost: *Realm of the Black Mountains: A History of Montenegro,* by Elizabeth Roberts, (Ithaca: Cornell University Press, 2007), and the slimmer *Montenegro: A Modern History* by Kenneth Morrison, (London: Palgrave Macmillan, 2009). Morrison adds new research since the 2006 independence referendum in *Nationalism, identity and statehood in post-Yugoslav Montenegro* (London: Bloomsbury, 2018).

From Council of Europe, Observation of the presidential election in Montenegro (15 April 2018), Election observation report, Doc. 14564, May 31, 2018, http://assembly.coe.int/nw/xml/XRef/Xref-XML2HTML-en.asp?fileid=24779&lang=en "As regards the election campaign, there were reported cases of the misuse of State resources and credible allegations of pressure on voters in favour of the ruling party candidate. The ad hoc committee pointed out that regrettably those problems were recurrent in Montenegro, as well as credible allegations of vote buying and hiring of public employees during the election period." Samir Kajosevic, "'Envelope' Affair Raises Suspicion over Montenegrin Party Funds," Balkan Insight, January 25, 2019, https://balkaninsight.com/2019/01/25/envelope-affair-raises-suspicion-over-montenegrin-party-funds-01-24-2019/ Politikon Network, "The Thin Line Between the Party and the State in Montenegro," December 14, 2016, https://politikon.me/2016/12/14/the-thin-line-between-the-party-and-the-state-in-montenegro/ and Radio Free Europe, "Ten million euros for the Prime Minister's brother," January 14, 2016, https://www.slobodnaevropa.org/a/deset-miliona-eura-bratu-premijera-mila-djukanovica/27488022.html (in Serbo-Croatian)

Samanth Subramanian, "Inside the Macedonian Fake News Complex," WIRED, February 15, 2017, https://www.wired.com/2017/02/veles-macedonia-fake-news/ Julian Borger, "Twitter deletes 20,000 fake accounts linked to Saudi, Serbian and Egyptian governments," The Guardian, April 3, 2020, https://www.theguardian.com/technology/2020/apr/02/twitter-accounts-deleted-linked-saudi-arabia-serbia-egypt-governments

Klāvs Sedlenieks, "Buffer culture in Montenegro: bratstvo, kumstvo and other kin-related structures," in *A life for tomorrow: Social transformations in South-East Europe*, Predrag Cvetičanin, Ilina Mangova, Nenad Markovikj eds. (Skopje: Institute for Democracy/Societas Civilis, 2015).

On the smaller gap between the sexes in STEM in many of the communist countries, see "Why half the scientists in some eastern European countries are women," *The Economist*, July 18, 2019, https://www.economist.com/europe/2019/07/18/why-half-the-scientists-in-some-eastern-european-countries-are-women Quentin Lippmann, Claudia Senik "Math, Girls and Socialism," *Journal of Comparative Economics* 46, no. 3 (May 2018)

Erik Messori, "Girls unwanted," Al Jazeera, March 8, 2018, https://www.aljazeera.com/gallery/2018/3/8/girls-unwanted-this-is-not-a-country-for-women Also see UN Women data on Montenegro: https://data.unwomen.org/country/montenegro

Garth Massey, Karen Hahn and Duško Sekulić, "Women, Men, and the 'Second Shift' in Socialist Yugoslavia," *Gender and Society* 9, no. 3 (June 1995). This is an excellent paper on where exactly Yugoslav socialism failed to 'liberate' women. "Women in socialist countries had made tremendous gains in many spheres of social and political life; yet, they remained dramatically underrepresented in political bodies and in the most prestigious professions and fields of higher education. As important, problems particular to women's experiences were addressed through protective legislation and social provisions designed to ensure that women remain responsible for spheres of social life defined as 'women's work.'" 359.

John Lechte on the thought of Julia Kristen in the *Times Literary Supplement* online series Footnotes to Plato is very good for novices and old hands alike (https://www.the-tls.co.uk/articles/julia-kristeva-thought-revolt/). The Wikipedia entry for Kristeva's term 'semiotic' and its relation to the mother is quite OK. I also stumbled on an intriguing York University PhD thesis by Mary J. Harrison in which, following in Kristeva's footsteps, she examines "the dilemma that for a girl to become a separate and thinking self she must at once identify with and repudiate her mother . . . A girl's capacity to think and symbolize begins in an infantile and conflicted relation to her mother," and this can affect the life of the mind in later years. (https://yorkspace.library.yorku.ca/xmlui/bitstream/handle/10315/28194/Harrison_Mary_J_2014_PhD.pdf?sequence=2&isAllowed=y)

The Milman Parry Collection of Oral Literature is available on the Harvard Library website. See also Adam Kirsch, "The Classicist Who Killed Homer," *The New Yorker*, June 14, 2021.

https://www.britannica.com/place/Montenegro/History

Radovan Karadzić had been a poet before the war in Bosnia, Nikola Koljević a Shakespeare scholar and Belgrade-based poet Matija Bećković remains an important figure in Serbian nationalism.

Biljana Jovanović, *Dogs and Others*, trans. John K. Cox, (London: Istros Books, 2019). Marina Abramović, *Walk Through Walls: A Memoir* (New York: Crown Archetype, 2016).

Lydia Perović, "When We Were Brothers: On the Writing of Daša Drndić," *Los Angeles Review of Books*, April 4, 2019.

CHAPTER 10

Mihailo Lalić, *Hajka* (Belgrade: Nolit, 1960). All the quotes in this chapter are in my translation.

J. M. Coetzee, *Elizabeth Costello* (New York: Vintage Books, 2004).

David A. T. Stafford, "SOE and British Involvement in the Belgrade Coup d'État of March 1941", *Slavic Review* 36, no. 3 (September 1977), Cambridge University Press.

A lot of English-speaking historians and journalists have taken an interest in the romance of the Serbian nationhood unfolding over the centuries. I won't list any of their work here. It's easy to find. Unavoidable, even.

Michael Ondaatje, *Warlight* (New York: Knopf, 2018).

Milovan Djilas, *Rise and Fall* (San Diego: Harcourt Brace Jovanovich, 1985). I've used the Croatian re-issue expertly introduced by Slavko Goldstein, *Vlast i pobuna: memoari* (Zagreb: EPH/Novi Liber, 2009).

A 1827 Romantic song cycle narrated by a spurned lover rambling through a snowy forest towards probable death, *Winterreise* is still probably the most performed cycle of the nineteenth century. Slavoj Žižek attributed some of its popularity in Germany to its resonance with the images and narratives of German soldiers marching through the snow in the two world wars. But Winter Journey is to be found in Lalić as well, among the Yugoslav partisans who can claim it in equal measure. Ian Bostridge wrote about Žižek's—and many other—takes on the song cycle in his book *Schubert's Winter Journey: An Anatomy of Obsession* (New York: Knopf, 2015).

Northrop Frye, *Anatomy of Criticism: Four Essays*, 15th ed. (Princeton: Princeton University Press, [1957] 2000).

Božena Jelušić, *Mitsko u Lalićevim romanima* (Podgorica: Kulturno-prosvjetna zajednica Podgorice, 2000).

CHAPTER 11

Lydia Millet, "Alice in familyland," *Globe and Mail*, September 23, 2006. Christian Lorentzen, "Poor Rose," *London Review of Books* 35 no. 11 (June 6, 2013).

Aleksandar Hemon, *My Parents: An Introduction/This Does Not Belong to You* (New York: MCD, 2019).

Alice Munro, *Runaway* (Toronto: Penguin Canada, 2005). Alice Munro, *Selected Stories* (Toronto: Penguin Canada, 1998).

CHAPTER 12

Further to the question of how the performing arts are changing in the Anglosphere, see Helen Lewis's piece on the demands by Arts Council England, the main National Theatre funder, for 'relevance' as the primary value in the theatre company's programming: "The State of the National: How Britain's biggest theater reflects the country's identity crisis," *The Atlantic*, January 3, 2020.

Milovojević is quoted in Valerie Hopkins's, "In Balkans, Britain rejoins battle for influence. Soft-power struggle with Russia hots up as West renews interest in region," Politico.eu, March 30, 2018.

Izabela Kisić, Seška Stanojlović, "Media in Post-Milosevic Serbia," a report for the Helsinki Committee for Human Rights in Serbia (at https://www.helsinki.org.rs/reports.html)

Daniela Brkić, "Media Ownership and Financing in Montenegro. Weak Regulation Enforcement and Persistence of Media Control," South East European Media Observatory, November 2015, https://www.rcmediafreedom.eu/Publications/Reports/Media-Ownership-and-Financing-in-Montenegro.-Weak-Regulation-Enforcement-and-Persistence-of-Media-Control

Reporters Without Borders: Montenegro, on https://rsf.org/en/montenegro.

"Serbia and Montenegro: Are judges protecting journalists or their aggressors?," Reporters Without Borders, July 2, 2020.

"Investigative journalist shot and injured in Montenegro: Olivera Lakić wounded outside her home in the country's second attack on a journalist in a month," *The Guardian*, May 9, 2018.

Dusica Tomovic, "Montenegro Probes Investigative Reporter for Drug Trafficking," *Balkan Insight*, April 15, 2016. Nina Ognianova/CPJ Europe and Central Asia Program Coordinator, "CPJ joins call for Montenegro to free imprisoned journalist Jovo Martinović," Committee to Protect Journalists, September 19, 2016. "RSF and its partners call on the Montenegro court to definitely acquit journalist Jovo Martinović" on rsf.org, October 5, 2020.

Hannah Lucinda Smith, "West must save free press before it's too late," The Times, August 14, 2020, https://www.thetimes.co.uk/article/west-must-save-free-press-before-its-too-late-mrndkpqmm

Sarah Rieger, "Advocates condemn xenophobic op-ed by Calgary instructor calling for end to diversity," CBC News, September 7, 2019. Cathy Young, "Israel and the Free Speech Problem. Did a Palestinian rights advocate get 'canceled' in Canada? Maybe, but the story also shows the limits of right-of-center 'cancel culture,'" ArcDigital, May 19, 2021. Susan G. Cole, "The show you won't see: Reena Katz and Koffler Gallery," NOW, June 3, 2009. Patrick Brzeski, "NBA's Apology to China Draws Outrage Across Political Spectrum," The Hollywood Reporter, October 6, 2019.

See Elizabeth Anderson's book *Private Government: How Employers Rule Our Lives (and Why We Don't Talk about It)* (Princeton: Princeton University Press, 2020), on the dictatorial nature of at-will employment.

Suzanne Moore, "Why I had to leave The Guardian," UnHerd, November 25, 2020. Kenya Evelyn, "Staff outraged at New York Times response to reporter's racist language," *The Guardian*, February 4, 2021. See also the *Blocked and Reported* podcast episode, "That Sinking, Racist Feeling When You've Lost The Newsroom," March 7, 2021. "The Toronto Star gets its moment of public dysfunction," The Line, August 26, 2020.

George Packer, "The Enemies of Writing," *The Atlantic*, January 23, 2020.

CHAPTER 13

The bit about the unruly polar bears in jail is true too. See Marcel Theroux, "Polar bears: close encounters of the furred kind in Canada," The Lonely Planet online, March 15, 2016.